MW01295629

The Science Of Flipping

By
Justin Colby

Copyright © 2014 Justin Colby

All Rights Reserved

MIH Publishing

Contents

Introduction

My business partner, Eddie Rosefield, and myself decided to create this book in order to help real estate investors, like you, successfully invest without the need to put your time in on the ground. We focus on providing the systems you can implement into your business that will enable you to keep from having to be on the job swinging the hammer yourself. In our business, we have excelled due to the creation and implementation of these systems. Now, we are sharing our knowledge in hopes that you too, can implement these systems into your flipping business and relieve yourself from having to physically by on your project site.

Real estate investors tend to spend too much time in their business, and not nearly enough time on their business. This book was written to help you develop a business model that will ideally allow you to flip homes while you are on vacation in another state, country, or from the comfort of your own home. Eddie and I sincerely want each and every one of you to have the life you desire. As you read through each chapter, you will realize that we are giving you the knowledge to implement some highly effective systems into your flip business that will enable you to work smarter, not harder.

Before we begin, let me tell you a little bit about what

Eddie and I have created at Phoenix Wealth Builders. For us, real estate investing hasn't always been a walk in the park, and I'm sure some of you may know that it isn't exactly puppy dogs and rainbows. In 2007, we started investing in Phoenix without even getting our feet wet – we just dove in headfirst.

Real estate investing had become our only source of income, and it took us 9 months to close our first deal. I don't know about you, but we were in no position to have paydays once every 9 months. Trust me, when I tell you that Eddie and I went through it…believe me! We understand what you may be going through as you get started in real estate investing. I would imagine that we faced some of the same hurdles you may be facing now or are going to encounter in the near future. Our first 16 months as real estate investors had only yielded us 2 deals. For us, that was hardly an income that we could actually live with.

Let's fast forward to 2012, when our company did 96 successful flips. In 2013, we managed to become developers, along with closing nearly 50 real estate deals. Our current development is a 79-unit townhome community on eight acres in Mesa, Arizona. With 4 of the 16 buildings up, and being open to the public less than a full month, we already have 2 contracts and the project continues to draw real interest and traffic. This is just one example of the type of success that you too, may have the opportunity to attain in your real estate investing experience by implementing our proven systems.

I have been a real estate coach for several years, and have worked with real estate investors from New York to California, and everywhere in between. No matter where my real estate students are located, the number one question I get asked is, "Where do I find the deals?" My students constantly say things like "I can't find any deals", "The auction has no more deals", "I can't find a deal on the MLS", "Wholesalers aren't getting good deals", and "They're all at retail prices." Does any of that sound familiar?

For a special welcome message and free bonus, visit

www.TheScienceOfFlipping.com

Secrets To Finding Deals In Today's Market

This chapter is focused on how to find deals in today's market. What tools can and should you use? What type of networking tactics can help you? To be honest, there are only two ways to find deals – by either networking or marketing. The key is to focus center your attention on the people who are actually doing deals in today's market. I have a great story for you that will illustrate this key point.

When I first moved out here to Arizona, my job was to meet every big real estate investor I could find in Phoenix. All I wanted to do was figure out who was really doing deals, who was really wholesaling deals, and who was really flipping deals and make sure they knew who we were. So I started asking around town.

I started calling real estate agents, and I would spend days at a time setting up meeting after meeting at a local Starbucks just to get a sit- down with them and talk to them about what we did. I had to ask a few simple questions like "Do you know anyone we can align ourselves with who possibly would be a good colleague to know in the area?" I'd offer help to them as well.

We spent day after day cold calling agents and building relationships. From those meetings we were introduced to several very large investors here in the Phoenix valley. I didn't do anything special; It wasn't that I used secret ninja tricks by any means. I simply went out each and every day doing grassroots networking.

From those meetings I started hearing about other meetings that were going on in our community. I discovered the REIA and other similar groups and started going to those meetings. From there I would do the same thing; I would simply network and let everyone know who I was and what we did here at Phoenix Wealth Builders. Eventually they would tell us about other people, other meetings, or other group events that I wanted to go to, and it just really built from there.

I spent a lot of my time networking, and that hasn't changed. Networking with people, getting to know them and understanding their needs is one of the most important factors in my success. If you just get out there and start networking, you'll be on your way to becoming a successful real estate investor. This is why I'd like to share some great networking resources that have helped my business partner and me meet companies and individuals who have had a huge impact on our lives.

Let's start with one of those resources located here in the West, specifically in Phoenix. Every single day there are auctions at the Trustee Auction Sale. Every morning there is a group of investors who go down there looking to buy fix-and-flip deals or possibly wholesale deals. One of the things I learned very quickly is that if we wanted to meet real investors, we had to get our butts down to the auction in Phoenix. Again, it happens every day.

No matter what position you are in, whether you have no money and no credit or a lot of money and good credit, getting to know those individuals will really mean a lot. Our intention initially was never to go down there to buy the homes; it was just to shake hands, exchange business cards, and get our name out there, let them know that we were looking to buy, fix and flip a couple of deals this year.

We didn't want to seem too ambitious, so we just wanted them to know that we were looking to buy our next deal and, if they did come across something, we could be a buyer for them. If they were looking to unload something relatively quickly they could give us a call, put us on their email list, shoot us a text message, and we would take a look at that.

We've had great success and have built relationships down at the auction to the point that in 2011 most of the homes we bought were from there. We worked with other investors as well, but we got so comfortable at the auction that by the end of 2011, I would say 90 percent of our deals came from there.

Some of the relationships we've created from the

auction are wholesalers. A lot of the people we've met down at the auction like to wholesale their deals. If they place the winning bid they will give us a call right then saying, "Hey, I've got this address, 123 Main Street, for $100,000. I'll sell it to you right now for $105,000." We just run out to the property, take a look at it, and run the numbers to feel out if it's something we would want. Since we're able to buy the wholesalers' properties, they'll now view us as their number one, go-to fix-and-flip investor they can sell deals to. No longer do we need to be on their buyers' list; they just shoot us a call right at the time they win the bid and say "Hey, do you want this deal?"

We have three or four investors we've met at the auction who do the same thing for us. Each time they close a deal, we get their first call. That has turned out to be one of the best ways for our business to continue moving forward. That networking alone gives us anywhere from 20 percent to 40 percent of the deals we will buy in a given year.

In 2013 we have really depended on wholesalers to find deals. A good portion of our deals have come from wholesalers in this market, and a good portion of the wholesalers we have developed relationships with have come from the auctions. Depending on where you are, auctions might be held every day. I really recommend showing up to those auctions every day they are being held, primarily to meet other investors, shake their hands, and get on their radar as a great way to network and find deals.

When we began we had no start-up capital, none. We went both feet in. We had no income, and I decided we were going to follow a grassroots strategy. I said to Eddie that our focus was going to be on meeting real estate agents all day, every day until we had five or ten agents ready to work with us, and that's what I did, just jumped online.

At that time we had no Multiple Listing Service (MLS) access. All we had were the free websites, so whether it was Red Fin, Craigslist, you name it, we jumped on it, simply calling the agents and asking for a coffee meeting. I would book my day from about 9 a.m. until late afternoon; I'd sit at that coffee shop and have meeting after meeting. Primarily I just offered the agents help, letting them know that we were investors and telling them what we were looking for, that we'd seen one of their listings and had a certain amount of interest in it, that we would like to work with them, to be a buyer for them and for them to utilize us as a buyer to get deals. It was very, very successful.

I did that for quite some time. I know not everyone has the time to sit at a coffee shop every day for two or three weeks and just meet realtors, but from that came three or four great realtors we started using. They leveraged us to get listings for themselves, and we leveraged them to put in offers for us on their listing. We could be their first offer on that listing as well as other listings they were getting or already had. We would put in a list of offers and they would simply make us a priority. Those days were fun. The days of simply networking, meeting people, and building relationships became awfully fruitful.

When you do network with someone, you start to realize they're thinking, "What's in it for me? How are you going to make this beneficial for me?"

If you always position yourself in that way and make a relationship beneficial for the other person, they'll want to work with you. They really will. If you don't have time to sit down at a coffee shop for hours at a stretch, make it one or two hours a day, or maybe just one or two a week. Whatever it can be, I highly suggest sitting down with real estate agents. Grab a cup of coffee and try to develop relationships with them.

Only three or four months ago we met with a young real estate agent here in Scottsdale, Arizona. He already had a successful business going, but he had heard of us and seen us buy a couple of deals. He wanted to take us out for coffee, so I sat down with him and from there we were able to buy.

We've now closed on three deals with him and plan on buying more. The point is that I've never stopped networking and never will stop, though I probably don't do it quite as much as I used to when we were first beginning because we now have a successful business up and running. But remember that networking is, in my opinion and that of my mentors, the number one way to get deals in this market.

One of the ideas I had a long time ago was to leverage relationships with title companies. Title companies do nothing but real estate transactions; the large ones do thousands of real estate transactions a month. I started building relationships with different title companies, for instance Fidelity National Title, Chicago Title, and First American Title.

I would go and meet with either their sales rep or a title agent I knew and build a relationship. The relationship would begin with, "We'd like to give you guys a couple of deals if we can. What are you looking for? What are your rates for title insurance?"

I would describe our business, what we focused on, what we did day to day, and then I would simply say, "Can you think of anyone who might be good for us to meet, whether it be a lender, contractor, real estate agent, loan broker, etc.?" I would just ask. You will be surprised what you get when you ask. People very rarely refuse to answer the questions or don't give you good answers. They will usually say, "I think it would be good for you to meet so-and-so," or "So-and-so is a top earner. As a real estate agent I think they would be right up your alley. I just did a couple of deals with them."

That has always been my secret ninja trick: I start leveraging title companies. A lot of people don't think to leverage them, but if you're able to do a deal or two they will give you as many people as you could ask for. If they think someone would be of value to you, they are happy to introduce you.

I still do this. Eddie and I recently went to a lunch meeting with two title reps (one was a sales rep for the title company; the other actually was the title rep). Because we're developers now, the meeting revolved around land acquisition deals. The title rep said, "Hey, I have a builder who has several pieces of land they're contemplating selling. Here's their information. Why don't you reach out to them? Let them know that you got their information from me and see if something comes from that."

I reached out to the builder, who gave me three pieces of property that we're currently looking at. Land acquisition is obviously not quite as quick as your typical residential fix-and-flip, but it is a potential for deals we will buy. There is one deal specifically that we are looking very closely at buying in the next 30 to 45 days. We're finishing up some due diligence and we may be on our second development project.

I'm telling you it's as simple as asking. It's as simple as networking. It's as simple as going to these companies and asking them, "Is there anyone you can think of that you think I should be introduced to?" Title companies hold meetings every single week. Many of their meetings are educational, but guess who's there? Other investors, other loan brokers. These meetings are a great way to network. Getting on the title companies' mailing lists will help you.

Most states and most cities also have Real Estate Investor Association (REIA) meetings, typically held once a month. Though they don't happen as often, these meetings are a great networking source. A lot of times people are there who are just getting started and want to learn more, but that's okay. They're worth building a relationship with. You can take that relationship and build your team with them because they're willing to get their hands dirty, or they might be a buyer for one of your wholesale flips or one of your traditional flips.

And REIA meeting contacts can be put on your buyers' lists. When you buy a home at auction, off the MLS, or from wholesalers, you send it out to your buyers' list, right? Flip the deal and get your quick nickel.

Let me reinforce this with a story. I called an investor I knew and suggested coffee. He started telling me about a deal and I was excited for him. He kept referencing who he had bought it from, so I said, "Who are they? Do you mind introducing me to this group?" He gave me their email and phone number and said, "Why don't you just reach out and let them know that I referred you to them?"

To this day, it is a wholesaling group that I still buy deals from. I've bought so many deals from them over the years that they text me before they even blast it out on their email, saying, "Hey, do you want this? Here's your first look." Right then and there I'm able to analyze it if I'm at my office and we make a decision. We've been able to gain that priority because we act quickly, but also because we actually buy their deals.

We're not tire kickers. If you do want to create great relationships while networking, focus on helping the person. You want to help them as much as you can, because ultimately if you help them you're going to end up getting what you want no matter what. When you are networking, always impress those individuals and always try to focus on how can you be helpful to them rather than how they can be helpful to you. You can call that karma. You can call it "putting it out in the universe." It is what it is. It always gets you to your goal.

Let's shift gears a little bit and start jumping into marketing. This is a very broad topic. In future sections you're going to hear more about in-depth styles of marketing, how to market, and where to market, but let's just cover marketing as a whole right now.

I'm a huge advocate of marketing for deals. Some people would say using the MLS and writing offers on the MLS is a great way to market because you're getting your name out there and listing agents are starting to see the same buyer over and over again, and I agree. I think if you're specifically going after a handful of agents and they see your name over and over again, they're going to start recognizing who you are and realizing you're a buyer who wants a deal. If you want to focus on those agents, then give them a call and let them know you're making offers so they know you're a real person, that you're really here to buy their listings. It's a style of marketing that's useful because real estate agents will call you and start finding you to say, "Hey, I'm about to get a listing." But there are many different ways to market.

A lot of my mentors have started with bandit signs; it's one of the oldest ways of marketing that you hear about. In fact I use bandit signs today in Phoenix, and they still work. The authorities will call and make you take them down or they'll just take them down themselves, so it starts to become a bit of pain to keep putting them back up and can be costly at times, but the fact is if you have proper placement, if you're in the right areas and are visible and people are taking a look, it absolutely works.

With bandit signs, you have to be creative. So many times you'll see the typical "We buy ugly houses" or

"Buy houses for cash" and that's fine, but you want to be a little bit more creative. I remember once I was walking by a bandit sign and the sign was written upside down, and so what did I do? I walked past it, realized it was written upside down, turned around, and went back to read it.

It caught my attention. I actually stopped and turned around to read it again. That is being creative. You really want to pop. Often a color will make you more noticeable, but no matter what marketing you're doing, you want to try to be as creative as possible. Gain as much attention as possible. Bandit signs are obviously a very good way of marketing.

Another great technique I still use today, and in my opinion is our strongest suit, is direct mail marketing. There are so many different types of sellers out there to mail to. You can be very specific and go by zip code; you can really whittle down a list to mail directly to these sellers. What we do is focus on nonlisted properties, those that don't have a real estate agent attached to them, and we send those sellers direct mail. They could be probate sellers. They could be going through a divorce. They could be losing their home to foreclosure. They could be inheritance sellers. They could just be high-equity sellers. They could be absentee sellers who don't live in the home. There are so many lists you can buy nowadays that you can mail to.

We happen to use an online database that scrapes the county records every two weeks to update itself, and that provides the list of motivated sellers we mail to. It works so well that last month we sent out just 200 mailers, a small amount, to a very specific area. We used a certain zip code; we did not do a blast mailer. From 200 mailers we got two deals. That is a very good rate of return on your investment. We get very specific with whom we are marketing to.

Again, I list a handful of people to market to and then we continue to do it. One of the main rules of marketing in direct mail specifically is that you have to be consistent. If you send out one mailer of 200, the example I just gave you, you can't just send it out once; you need to send it out to the same people a minimum of three times. Once you've sent it out at least three times and gotten no return, that's good enough to move on from that group. You have to be very consistent and repetitive in your mailing.

Online marketing is huge right now. So many people believe in online marketing, me included. There are so many different avenues of online marketing that it can get a little overwhelming; there's a lot out there, and I understand that. I'm not the most techie person in the world—I tend to leave it to other people in our business to control the Internet side—but marketing on Craigslist is a huge advantage.

We have pulled sellers off of Craigslist.

Let people know that you buy homes or that you are looking. A lot of times you can do a role reversal or reverse your methodology. You say you're looking to sell a home so buyers will then call you. When you reach a buyer, you actually want to get added to their buyer's list so that when they get a home, you're on their list. Getting on a buyer's list is always a good opportunity.

Social media and online marketing arehuge right now. I strongly recommend that if you don't have a great understanding of it, start looking into it. I know the times have changed and many of you began investing years ago before Facebook and LinkedIn and Twitter and all these social media sites were even thought of, but it's something you're going to have to learn because that's where the real estate industry is going. Craigslist, Facebook, LinkedIn, and other social media work like a charm. Start utilizing Facebook, start utilizing LinkedIn, start utilizing Twitter, because deals come from them. If nothing else, it's a great way to network.

Lastly, I want to focus on a subject that is close to my heart. Some people will take a look at deals, and they do find deals but then make the argument that they're not deals. It all depends on how you're looking at that property. First and foremost, never let anyone else tell you the value of that home, ever. Always do your own research.

What more investors need to do and what will take your business to the next level is readdressing how you look at the home. Adjust the goggles you're viewing that specific home with.

I'll give you a very good example. We bought a home that was a 3-1. Typically we stay away from 3-1, but this one happened to be in a very good area. Normally we would have just looked at the fact that it was a 3-1, stopped there and said we didn't want it, but we looked at the area and thought, "Okay, that's a great area." It was in Arcadia, which is a very affluent area here in Phoenix, and we wondered, "How can we make this a deal?" We looked at adding on a bathroom. What we had to do then was figure out the dollar per square foot to build and then the actual rehab budget, and then figure out if there was any room to do that. The focal point is to change how you run your comps, how you're analyzing the deal, because no longer are you simply looking for comps of 3-1; you're now looking for comps of 3-2.

The way we're looking at specific deals is changing, and I think right now that's everyone's focus: how you can find deals in today's market. Between Eddie and me, we've coached thousands of students across the country, and everyone gives the same argument: "We can't find deals."

Change the glasses that you're looking at those deals with. Instead of saying there are no comps to support a deal, start looking at it with possible added square footage. Put on a bedroom, put on a bathroom, add a pool. Add to the home so that the comps no longer are a 3-1 or even a 3-2. Add a bedroom and you have 4-2 comps. Sometimes that makes the deal a home run, sometimes it doesn't. Sometimes it doesn't matter what you do it is just not a deal, and that's okay, but this is how you take your business to the next level.

This is how you take your business from two deals a year to six deals a year, or from 10 deals a year to 20 deals a year. In our business here in Phoenix we went from 46 deals to 96 deals, and we did it by readjusting the way we were looking at properties.

Start adjusting how you're looking at these listings, how you're looking at the homes down at auction, how you're looking at the homes being sent to you from wholesalers, and adjust what you would do to those homes.

One of the things that a very successful investor here in Phoenix does is to focus on homes he can tear down and rebuild. Completely rebuild, not just rehab but rebuild. That is another way to look at a specific deal. If you think, "The home is too walled. I don't buy homes in that age range," maybe again, adjust how you're looking at that.

Maybe you're not necessarily buying that home for rehab but to tear down to build a brand-new home. Now that brings you into a slightly different category; you've got to figure out what it's going to cost you per square foot to build. But again, I hear over and over, "There are no deals out there. I can't find a deal." In my opinion, put on a different set of glasses and adjust how you're looking at it.

Raising Private Money For Your Deals

This chapter is about raising private money. This subject is very close to my heart and I'm very passionate about it, because this is what I do. I'm going to show how you can take your business from doing two deals a year to six deals a year raising private money. Get excited because this is a great topic.

In our business, a lot of times I'll take on the creative side, but the number one rule, regardless of whether you're a real estate investor or another type of investor, is that you always want to leverage other people's money.

OPM. You've heard it over and over again, I know. We've taken that to heart, read countless books, listened to countless people speak about it. We have friends in the banking industry as well as the financial industry, and time and time again they talk about using other people's money. It's what you do when you buy a home for yourself to live in: you get a bank loan. It's not always your money. You leverage your money with other people's money. Yes, a bank is an institution, but nonetheless you're using their money rather than your money.

When you're thinking about raising private money, there's no right or wrong way to do it. I was on stage for about eight hours Saturday teaching a group of 25 or 30 investors who'd come all the way from Pennsylvania to California, and I spoke in depth about this subject. I took tons of questions about how to structure certain deals.

There's no right or wrong, but at this point we prefer to take certain money structures on. We no longer like to take on the 50-50 deal in which it's a joint venture, they provide the money and you run the rehab. I'm not going to tell you that you should not do that, but I will say that at this point we like rate-of-return money. We like 8 percent to 10 percent money, structured so that we can pay them quarterly or annually or possibly when a deal closes. That's what we do today.

But these 25 or 30 real estate investors I was talking to had multiple questions about situations in which they might have a deal but no money and they have a potential lender for that deal, and they asked me how to structure it. How do I present it to the lender?

Let's start there. That's the number one key to raising private money: You need to have a certain presentation. We've raised private money a number of different ways, but let's just use the example that you have friends and family who have a decent amount of money. It might be in CDs, it might be in their IRA, but let's say your parents, your grandparents, your aunt, your uncle, or your friends have money sitting somewhere and you could get them a better rate of return. Well, how do you go to them? What are you structuring? How are you presenting it to them so they can see this as an actual value and want to invest their money with you to get a certain return?

First of all, let's start by talking about what kind of return they're currently getting. If they're in a bank somewhere or have a CD or an IRA, they're getting 1, 2, 3, or I think 4 percent is the highest it gets nowadays. I'm not a financial adviser, but I know the banks aren't giving you a ton of interest back. When I had my CDs, which I no longer have because they were nothing, I think I was making close to 3 percent, which nowadays is not much money.

There are ways obviously now that I invest my money in real estate with which I get a much higher percent. Let's talk about how you're going to present them with an opportunity to also make a higher return than they're currently making. Maybe do a little due diligence. Maybe ask the friends and family about what they're getting as a return. Are they interested in making a higher return?

Now you need to figure out what type of return would push them over the edge to lend money to you. Is it 8 percent, 6 percent? I've found in doing this for as long as I have that most lenders now won't lend for less than 8 percent. Traditionally you're probably going to be a little bit closer to 10 percent or 12 percent as a rate of return, but then you can structure your money in a certain way. If you're able to get a lower interest rate, you may be able to offer them some points on the front end. To use $100,000 as an example, if you're getting 8 percent you may be able to say, "I'll pay you a point or two on the front end so I can get an 8 percent loan." If you're paying a point or two, you're paying a $1,000 or $2,000 up front so that you have 8 percent in case you have to hold that home for a little bit longer.

Now there are multiple ways to structure this deal. Again, utilizing the idea that you're speaking to a friend, a family member, a close colleague, someone that you know, you need a certain presentation. If you know these individuals, you know exactly how want to present. What's going to push them over the edge? I suggest you start with your ideal scenario, because if you're able to pitch up, they might accept it. They may take you up on that. They might take the 10 percent because they're only getting 3 percent in the CD or whatever else their money is invested in. Come to the table with a presentation saying, "I have a deal here. It looks like we're going to be able to buy it at $100,000, put about $30,000 or $35,000 into it and sell it for close to $200,000. We're looking to borrow money at 10 percent interest. Would you be willing to invest with me? You would be making 10 percent. I would be doing the rehab and we would pay you monthly," or quarterly, annually, however that may be structured.

You need to go to them, whoever that lender may be, and right now we're just speaking to friends and family or close colleagues. You need to present it to them as what's in it for them. At the end of the day, lenders only care about two things: one, what's in it for me, meaning how much money am I going to make; and two, how am I protected? It's not really an "or," it's an "and": what's in it for me and how am I protected? You need to present those two things.

The way we protect here in Phoenix is simply by deed of trust and a promissory note. The deed of trust is recorded by the title company, and the promissory note is held in a file, signed off by both me, the borrower and the lender, and then that gets recorded in the file as well. Now I have a promissory note saying, "I promise to pay you back what you lent me." Again, formalize that presentation.

Now maybe you don't have a deal. Maybe you're working on just raising the money first because you feel like you need to have the money before you can even go get a deal. Well, in that case your presentation may be a little bit different. You don't have a deal to entice them, right? The argument now amounts to what comes first, the chicken or the egg? You can make an argument for both.

I've raised money in both ways, where we had a deal and said, "Hey, we need $100,000. Will you lend on this deal?" and also just saying, "We're doing five to ten deals a month. We need $500,000. Will you lend us as a company the $500,000, on which we will pay you 10 percent interest quarterly?" I've done both of them. Both of them work. It depends on how you are looking at it.

Let's use the example where you're going to your friends, family, or close colleague and simply saying, "We're going out here to flip deals. We want to flip two deals before this year's over. We're currently in the ninth month, which gives us three more months in the year, and we're looking to flip one or two deals. Price point is going to be $100,000 to $150,000. Rehab is going to be close to $30,000 or $40,000 per home. The returns are going to look like this. What do you say about giving us a loan for 10 percent interest, paid quarterly, and putting your money at a title company in a loan toward my company, Phoenix Wealth Builders?"

Here's the thing: everybody in the world knows about real estate. Why is that? Because no matter what channel you go to on TV, there is a real estate program showing you how to flip deals, how to buy from the auction, how to renovate your kitchen, how to do it yourself, how to take a backyard from nothing to something. Every single channel now has something to do with flipping homes, and that's great for us.

I have raised so much money leveraging people's

excitement about flipping deals, their excitement about real estate. This market has been in a craze over the last 18 months; it's a great time to get in real estate because the market is going up. You want to be aware of how much it's going up and how long it's been going up for. Obviously because of the crash several years ago you have to be aware of that, but it is a great time to get into real estate because right now you can buy a deal, hold it for two months and sell it for a profit.

Right now everyone's excited about it and I leverage everyone's excitement. I leverage people watching all these shows about flipping homes and buying from the auction and doing the rehabs yourself and whatever else is out there. They're excited about it, so I say, "You want to be a part of it? This is what we do."

You'll get that golden nugget. If you're looking to get your first deal, it may take a little bit of time. It may require your gaining trust from them. You might need to leverage someone you know who's currently doing this by saying, "These are my partners." You may need to give a little bit more money than you originally wanted if this is the first time you've raised money, or the first time you're raising money to flip homes. You might have to do that, but formulate your presentation first. What are you going after and what is the rate of return you're seeking? Always start at your ideal situation. You don't have a house; you're looking just to get a loan at 10 percent.

What happens if they say, "You know what, I'm really not looking to be a lender on this deal. I'm really not looking to just lend you money, but what do you think of maybe partnering on a deal?" Okay, I'm of the opinion that you've got to take that money if you can. Here's the thing: I would prefer to take 50 percent of something than 100 percent of nothing. When we first started, I had lender after lender say, "I'm not really looking to just be a lender. I want to be a part of it."

Then you get creative, because you don't want to go all the way to "Let's do a deal 50-50" right away. Don't go there yet. Say, "Okay, why don't we put a spin on this? Why don't we give you an either/or? Give us a loan at 10 percent or take 15 percent of the profit, whichever is greater." Now they have an option. Now they can technically look at it as either "The 10 percent would give me more return" or "The 15 percent of the profit is going to give me more return."

Now they're a part of the deal. Now you're psychologically giving them the idea that they're flipping a home as well. That gets people excited. I was on stage all day Saturday teaching this group of investors, and time and time again, I was asked this question about a certain deal and certain creative financing, I would say, "What's going to get them excited about it?" The answer is they want to feel they're a part of something. If you need to spin it and offer them possibly 15 percent saying, "Give me a loan at 10 percent or at 15 percent of the deal," that pushes people off the fence.

That gets them excited, because you're going to talk about the homes you're looking to buy.

Again, you're raising the money first. You don't have a home yet, but you're going to give them the presentation about "I'm looking to buy in this price point. The rehabs are going to be this price and we're going to sell there. I buy for $100,000, I put $30,000 into it, I sell it for $200,000." You've got to lay that out for them, and then you get them excited by saying, "We'll give you 15 percent of the profit or we'll give you 10 percent of interest on your money, whichever is greater."

A lot of people, and I'm one of them, did not get into real estate investing because we had rich friends and family. We didn't have a dime to our name. Remember our story: when we started we went both feet in. Ed quit his job; I stopped being a real estate agent, and we went both feet in to real estate investing.

I told you guys it took us nine months to get our first deal done. Nine months is a long time to go with no income. We didn't do that because we knew our uncle was super rich and would lend down some money or that we had family with a bunch of investment properties and knew we could get a deal done right away. We didn't start investing because of that; we started investing because we wanted something more for ourselves. We wanted to create a lifestyle for ourselves beyond what we currently had. We had a vision of where we could go and we stuck to that.

Now let's talk about going after someone you don't know. How do you find them? Where do you go to find a lender who doesn't know you from Adam? I'm telling you, this is the fun part to me. This is where I start getting creative. Let's start with how you find someone you don't know who would possibly lend.

There are public records that you have access to; it doesn't matter what state you're in. Whether you're in Florida, New York, California, or Kansas, there are public records that say who is lent on a deal. Go to the county recorder's office and it will pull up who is lending money on on a deal, and there are databases you can buy a list from of private lenders who have recorded a deed on a property.

This is who you want to focus on. There are databases and list providers and title companies that can get you that list. That list is what you then use to direct mail to those people. What's on your piece of direct mail could simply be something like "I saw you lent on property 123 Main Street. We're looking at buying a property right near there. Would you be interested in lending again? If you are, please contact me at [your email address] or [your phone number]." That's as simple as it can be, and we do this here in our business in Phoenix every single month. We do this even though we have millions and millions of dollars to use in our fix-and-flip business. We never want to stop; we always want more money so our business can be bigger.

Eddie and I don't come from families with a lot of money, we don't have friends that have a lot of money, and we don't have a lot of colleagues we can ask for a loan, so we started by using direct mail. The funniest thing about that is the direct mail has given us a return of millions of dollars.

I have a story about how we sent out a piece of direct mail to a group; I think we did 500 at a time. One of those people happened to be in California and he gave us a call based off the mailers. We had a 20- or 30-minute conversation.

He said, "What do you do? How do you do it? What have you done over the last little while? Okay, this is what I do: I've lent privately on close to 300 homes out there in Arizona. I have a big-time investor who is flipping homes out there and has been for 10 years, so I've been his lender and I'm looking to lend some more money. Why don't you find a deal and send it over to me? I'll do a very quick analysis of it, and if I like what I see I'll lend you guys money. Not only will I lend you guys money, but I'll lend you 100 percent of the money."

How awesome is that? I didn't know this gentleman. His name is Tony, by the way. I just met Tony for the first time last month. After doing deals upon deals, after borrowing millions of his dollars, I just met him for the first time last month. How cool is that? Think about that. I never knew him, never met him. He wired us the first deal. He said, "Here are the terms. If you're good with that, I'll wire the money the second you're ready to close." He wired two days before we were closing. Title had the money, we were set to close, we closed the deal: easy.

I tell you guys that because a lot of you are probably asking, "How do you get the deal?" I'm going to be an advocate of direct mail. How do you get that lender? Go find them from the list. The list providers, the MLS; make use of MLS and go find it. There are databases; we use a database here. This is how we raised millions and millions of dollars, and we don't ever stop. We can never have enough money. That's how we find them.

There are several other ways to find lenders. Putting up Craigslist ads is one. Networking is another. I bring up networking all the time. I ingrain it into these podcasts because this has been so helpful for our business. We have gone to the REIA meetings. We have gone to the title company meetings. We have gone to the real estate agents meetings. We have gone to real estate seminars. We have paid probably close to $100,000 worth of real estate education, but out of that real estate education we have found lenders.

You can never be too creative in finding money. What about financial advisers? What about lawyers? These are people who deal with individuals every single day. Financial planners, financial advisers—people who are in charge of other people's money tend to have a lot of money and to have people they know who would lend on real estate. Maybe you start a campaign to financial planners or advisers or possibly lawyers. These are people who know people. They may even become your lender.

I'll give you another great story. I've actually been able to utilize a buyer, one of our own buyers who comes in and buys properties to hold as rentals, and he ended up being a private lender for us. How did that happen? Well, he came into town, we drove him around, we showed him some homes; he wanted to buy a couple of rental homes. He's from Colorado. He loves Phoenix as a great place to buy rental properties. We had some lunch with him and I simply asked him, "Listen, I understand you're buying a lot of these homes cash. Have you ever thought about lending to investors, someone like me? Have you ever thought about that?"

He said, "No, I never really thought about that," and I said, "Well, you're buying these homes and you're getting an 8 percent cap rate." Which is basically saying that after he pays everything out and pays off the taxes and the overhead of holding that home, his rent gives him an 8 percent return on his money. So I said, "Hey, I think I'd be willing to give you a 10 percent return consistently on your money; would you be open to that?" He said, "Absolutely!" Next thing you know, he wired us $100,000 and we had an extra $100,000 to do two deals. We did two deals with him and he loved it. He got his return. We gave him all his money back plus his interest. He loves us; he thinks we are the best investment he's ever made and now he's looking to do more.

You can find lenders anywhere. You can take a buyer and turn them into a lender. There's no right or wrong way to find the money. When you have someone you don't know, you've got to look at it again: do you have a deal you can present them? Because it all goes back to your presentation. I just gave you the story of the lender out in California who said, "Present me the next deal you guys are going to buy. I'm going to take a quick look at it." He is advanced, he has experience in lending deals, but what if someone doesn't? Then you need to put a presentation together.

If they don't know you and they don't have experience in lending, you have to do the work for them. Don't expect them to understand what you're talking about. I have a current lender here in Phoenix who has never been a lender before. I've spent a lot of time getting him to understand how lending works and how it will work specifically with us, so that when the next deal comes around, he's ready to pull the trigger.

Realize that it takes time, especially when you're dealing with someone who has never lent before or someone who doesn't know you. You're going to have to put in time to raise the money.

Again I want to go back to the subject of being creative in figuring out how you're going to borrow their money. I would present my best circumstance. How do I really want it? I want 10 percent flat. I'll pay them monthly or quarterly or at the end of the year, or at the end of the deal, but I just want to give them a flat interest rate similar to banks. That's how I now structure our money.

That wasn't always the case. Again, it wasn't always puppy dogs and rainbows. We had to take whatever money we could when we could, so we had to do joint venture deals, but I'm an advocate of saying I would rather have 50 percent of something than 100 percent of nothing. If you have to get to that 50 percent point, if you have to partner with someone, do it. Absolutely do it. Get your first deal under your belt or get two deals done at the same time.

Leveraging is key right now. I'm a huge advocate of leveraging. Whether you can do one deal or 10 deals, leverage other people's money. I was just talking to a student after I was on stage and he pulled me out to the corner to ask me a couple of questions. He was using his money to buy all his deals, and I said, "Okay, that's not a huge problem, but I'm not an advocate of that. Why don't you go find someone else's money to buy your deals, and if you want, use your money to buy more deals? Why don't you take the 14 deals you're working on that have your money in them right now and find a lender to buy you out of those deals at 10 percent?"

This individual happens to have good credit, a high net worth, and a good income; he could probably get a bank to give him a line of credit, which is what I suggested he do: Use someone else's money and then take your money and do more deals if you have the bandwidth. This is all about creating systems. If he doesn't have the systems, he's not going to be able to do more deals. He's not going to be able to do 28 deals to the 14 he's doing right now if he doesn't have the systems. He's going to have to create those systems, and I told him I'd work with him on that. He's one of our students and is already doing 14 deals, but I told him leverage is key right now. In this economy, while the market is going up, this is when you want to leverage other people's money.

Again, let's get back to the point that there's no right or wrong way to get a deal done. Whether you're presenting this to your family or to a lender you don't know, if you need to offer them a joint venture situation, if you need to offer them a partnership agreement so they can get a percentage of the deal, do it, but don't sell yourself short. You have to understand that people love 10 percent money right now. They will take 10 percent of their money all day long, so start there. If you have to go to 15, go to 15. If you have to go higher, you might need to build them into the deal.

They may need to be a percentage owner and get equity out as far as profit sharing. They may need to have 15 or 20 percent of the profit. I don't suggest going much more than 15 percent, because there's a hard-money lender somewhere near you who will do the deal at 18 percent. There's tons of hard money out there, and in another chapter you're going to be reading about the difference between hard money, private money, and conventional money through banks.

It's okay to give away part of the deal so you can get it done. I'm passionate about this and I can go on and on about it. It does not matter whether you find the home first or you raise the money first. The question is whether it's the chicken before the egg. What are you more comfortable doing? Are you more comfortable presenting a lender with a deal you already have lined up, or are you more comfortable saying, "I need money before I line up a deal; I'm not able to go get that deal until I have money ready to pull the trigger." Either way is fine.

We choose to find the deal first, because if the deal is really a deal, if it's really that good, you're going to go find that money. There's plenty of money out there that will do the deal if it's good. If you have a deal and it's good, send it to me. I'll do the deal. I'll lend the money. I'll JV with you. I'm saying there is money out there; it's closer than you think. There's no right or wrong way to do that.

It's really your preference. If you feel like you've got to raise that money, then raise the money, but don't sell yourself short. Don't try to raise money at a 50-50 profit split right away. Understand that you're willing to do it; know that that is in your arsenal and you can say, "Okay, guys, I'll do this deal with you at 50-50," but start at 10 percent. Start at 8 percent; shoot, start at 6 percent—why not? You never know what some people are willing to accept.

If your focus is to raise the money first, if it's a case of "I don't feel comfortable doing this unless I'm raising the money first; then I can go get a deal," you need to talk to your friends, family and colleagues. You need to network. Get out there and go to the auction, go to the REIA meetings, go to the title companies, and network with real estate agents. Simply ask questions like "Do you know of people lending money?"

If you don't do that, another great way to find private money is simply to send direct mailers out. Again, there are list providers and databases that have that information. MLS has it. You can find the lenders who record a private deed of trust, who have promissory notes on deals. That is all public information. Buy a list, utilize a database, and send out mailers. They absolutely work, and you will be shocked at how many people lend in your area.

If you're someone who says, "I need to find the deal first before I can even raise that money," okay, that's a little bit more what I do. I'm going to go find the deal, because if it's really a deal I'll be able to find money, period. It could be 10 percent money, partnership money, or JV money. Maybe give them the option: you can make 10 percent on your money or 15 percent of the deal or maybe 20 percent of the profit. Then go get the deal first, because now you have a clear, concise presentation to those people.

Here's what I would suggest, if you're going to go get the deal first. Get the deal but also be looking for the money. Put your feelers out: "Are you looking to get money? Are you looking to get in real estate?" Everyone wants to be in real estate now. It's all over the TV. I promise you, you will be shocked at how by just your asking if they want to be in real estate, if they want to look at lending on money, if they want to do any of that, people will say, "Yeah, what have you got? Let me see what you've got."

I'm not going to claim that you can make one call and go raise a million dollars. You might be able to make one call and raise $20,000, but you're going to need more money than that. Realize that even though I'm telling you where to go find it, it's going to require that you take the action. You'll hear that over and over again: you need to be the one taking action and pushing forward every day. Don't expect results if you're not going to put in the work. You've got to put in the work to get results. You need to send out the mailers, go to the networking meetings, go down to the auction. You need to call your family and call your friends. That's what's going to help.

I'm going to end with this great story about how we raised our first fix-and-flip money. This is something you can do, because you never know who you're talking to. The way Eddie and I raised our first $100,000 to do our first true fix-and-flip was, we were at a 49ers game. We were throwing the ball around and I heard my name called: "Hey Colby!" I looked around and it was one of my friends' friends. He knew me, we were mutual acquaintances, and he said, "Hey, your buddy Coleman's right over here. Quit throwing the ball around; why don't you come and say hi?"

I went over and said hi to my longtime buddy. We'd been friends for years but we'd just kind of lost contact. He was doing well and was a fireman. He was at the 9ers game; we loved the 9ers and we were just shooting it, and he said, "What are you guys up to nowadays?" I introduced him to my business partner, Eddie, and said we were flipping homes down in Phoenix, that we'd gotten a couple of homes done; it was awesome, fun, exhilarating, and I just talked it up because we were excited.

At this point I think we finally had our first two deals done and we were excited about where we were going, and I was just talking. I didn't really think about him being a private lender but just started talking about my business, about what we were going to do, about the goals we were setting for ourselves, and he got excited and said, "Hey, that's awesome. I just got this large inheritance. I have no idea what to do with it. Why don't we talk next week and let's talk business?"

I said, "Let's do that, let's talk business." So we all had a good time and went to the game, and I went over to his house a week after and he said, "Listen, I need to invest my money somewhere. I trust you; I've known you for years. Let's figure out a way that I can lend you some money." I said, "Not a problem. Let's write up a contract that you're going to lend us money at 10 percent interest. How much are you looking to lend?" He said, "$100,000." I said "Not a problem." We put up a contract, got it notarized, recorded it, and he lent us $100,000 that week.

That is how we raised our first $100,000. I didn't do

anything that you can't do. All I did was start talking about our business and how I was excited about it, and it got him excited about it. Right time, right place, the stars were aligned. Whatever you want to say, but I was simply talking to a good friend about what we were doing and he happened to be the one who had the money. Now guess what: because he loves what we do, he started telling people. That's the easiest way to raise money. Do good by others and they'll tell other people about it. Trust me when I tell you that.

I'll end this chapter by saying that there's no secret to what we do. The way we raised the first $100,000 was simply talking to a buddy with excitement about what we were doing. From there it just took off. We started doing mailers and raised another $100,000. We found a group out of California that was looking to lend some more money and partner on some deals and we would be the feet on the streets, so we partnered on a couple of deals. They brought the money, we brought the deals, and we partnered. Then the boyfriend of a friend of ours had some interest in it.

We started talking; he raised some money. He sent us a quarter of a million dollars.

We're not doing anything that you can't go do. If you don't have a lot of money to put out direct mail, network like crazy. Talk about what you're doing with excitement because then people will get excited about what you do. Get out there. You're going to have to spend something: you're going to spend your time or you're going to spend your money or both. Figure out which one you're willing to do.

Great Teams Build Great Businesses

This chapter will teach you how to build your team: how to find your team, where to find your team, whom you need on your team. If you want to be a successful investor, you can't do it alone. You can do a couple of flips a year or maybe even 10 deals a year, but you need a team around you to truly become a successful investor. We've done a very, very good job with it, and these days we're in meetings all day with our team, from realtors to contractors to real estate agents, everyone you can imagine.

This chapter will review how to build your team, which is part of the systems we're helping you implement to live the life you want to live. That's why we're putting this book out there. We want you to spend as much time on vacation with your family as you want, spend as much time with your friends as you want. We all want to live a certain lifestyle, and real estate investing is how we're creating the means to do it. We're here to teach you how to create those systems to live the lifestyle you truly want, whether you want to work five hours a day or you're the type of personality who wants to work 10 hours a day or maybe just 10 hours a week

I mentioned previously that to be successful in this business, to really build a business of real estate investing, you need to have the right people around you. You're only as good as your team. There are plenty of slogans out there about teamwork, and you hear it all the time: teamwork makes the dream work.

I truly believe it. Eddie and I started out back in 2007 with a dream of becoming successful real estate investors, and we worked as a team to get there. Between him and me, we worked and developed a larger team, which includes real estate agents, bird dogs, contractors, lenders, and private money lenders. It includes lawyers, accountants, web guys, social media guys, assistants, you name it—we have built that around ourselves so that our company has the team to push forward no matter what economy we might be in.

The first thing you have to decide is who you're looking for. If you're a rookie investor you might simply be looking for a good real estate agent to work with or possibly your first private money lender or your first contractor to work with. If you're a little bit more experienced and you have a contractor, maybe you're looking to get two or three contractors so that you can get multiple bids in order to get the best price on your rehabs. Maybe you're looking to raise more money; maybe you're looking for bigger and better agents. Maybe you're looking for a buying agent or another selling agent. Maybe you're looking for someone to build a website that really represents you.

First ask yourself, what team member do I need? Maybe

it's multiple team members, but you need to figure out what is the team member I need right now. Back when we first started, Eddie was working hard at the computers looking at the listings and figuring out what was a deal and what wasn't a deal, and I told him what I was going to do was grassroots marketing.

I was going to call these agents that we liked and set up meetings so that we could have a couple of handfuls of agents to represent us as buyers; that was what I was going to focus on. So I went down to Starbucks and filled my days with meetings, and out of that we found a great realtor. That realtor not only became a great buying realtor but also a great listing realtor.

Right then we actually filled two of our roster spots. We wanted a representation realtor who would go out there and represent us on the buyable; we also wanted someone, once we got a home, to list it to sell. After meeting upon meeting, I finally found the right fit. And then he met Ed and Ed said he was the right fit; then Ed and I met and we just said, "He's going to be the guy that's willing to put in the work to get us a deal or two. I know he's willing to put in that work."

That happened in the first four, five, or six months and we still didn't get a deal. This was the time of the short sale; if you were around then, you know the banks didn't know what they were doing. Heck, no one knew what they were doing back in those times, real estate or short sales. At that time it wasn't a novel idea, but the volume of short sales was crazy and no one knew how to negotiate them, and the banks didn't have anything in place to handle them. Still, we had an awesome real estate agent who put in the time and effort to make these offers for us, to work hard, and we finally made some money. That was our first team member.

Okay, now we've got a deal, who the heck is going to rehab that? How do you find that person? Let's focus on that question. At this point, how do you find who you're looking for? How do you find your assistant? How do you find a contractor? How do you find the right title company? How do you find the right real estate agent? There are a lot of different ways you can go out and find them.

Let's just bring up real estate agents.

As you heard, my technique back when we were just getting started was simply to cold call real estate agents who I saw had listings. We would jump on Zulu and just start calling these real estate agents. They didn't know who we were; they were probably thinking to themselves, "Who's this guy? What are they all about?" But that's what we did; we just called the real estate agents who had listings.

What happened in those meetings was I asked them a bunch of questions, they asked us a bunch of questions. I also asked questions about who their team consisted of.

Did they have contractors? Did they have good title representation? Who was their broker? Who did they typically use for lenders? Who was their preferred lender? I asked all these real estate agents these questions, and lo and behold, one of the agents I met did some work for us; I think one or two deals. He gave us a great lender and a great contractor before we even did a deal with him. We were using his contractor and lender even before he got paid on one of our deals.

First and foremost, when you are taking a meeting, no matter whether it's a title company, a lone broker, a real estate agent, or a contractor, ask them about who their team is. Do they have anyone good to refer to you? Frankly, that's how I found some of the best contractors we've had over the years.

The contractor is another great team member who is crucial in our business. Crucial. Where do you find contractors? Again, simply ask for a referral. Maybe your friends or family have great contractors who have done some work for them. Maybe your real estate agent has a good contractor they've worked with before. Maybe another investor you've networked with before has a good contractor.

I'll tell you a story. I bring these guys up a lot because they're investors here in Phoenix that we've worked with very closely; they're actually a wholesaler for the most part. Well, one day our contractor walked off three projects at one time. He had a personal meltdown.

We didn't know what was going on, but there were things happening in his life that he couldn't handle anymore, and he actually walked off three jobs that he was working on at the same time.

What did I do? I figured I had a bunch of real estate investing friends and colleagues, so why didn't I give them a call and see if they had a contractor to finish these jobs? I gave them a call. Right away one of them said, "You should call Luis; his number is this, and you need to talk to him and see if he can finish these projects for you."

The first thing I wanted to know was whether Luis was licensed here in the state of Arizona. He was, and right away he said, "I'm a little busy right now but I think I'll be able to finish these three jobs for you in the next four to five weeks." We got delayed, but the job got finished. We sold the homes and we made a profit, but the point is I just asked a fellow colleague, a fellow investor. To whom some people would view as competition, I just said, "Hey, I'm in a bit of a pinch. Do you have a contractor you've worked with who could help us out?" And he did it.

From the outset, always ask for referrals. Contractors: again, where would you find a contractor? Probably down at Lowe's or Home Depot. You walk in those places and you see some people with paint on them or they've got little wood chips on their hair—guess what, they're probably working on a home. Why don't you go up to them, introduce yourself, let them know who you are and what you're looking for, and see if they'd be interested in you buying them a cup of coffee sometime to talk about business. That's where I would probably start.

The next thing would be real estate agents, title companies. If you're driving down a street one day and you see a home is being worked on, don't be scared to go up in there. Ask who's running the job, who's the general contractor. See if you can get a name and see if you can take them to coffee.

Who else do you want on your team?

I gave you the examples of the realtors I first called. One of our main, top, best team members that we have right now is Michael, our realtor. He works with us in the same office, sublets one of our office spaces. He works with us every day. What he does is not to focus on our acquisitions but on our sales. We give him each and every listing.

How did we find Michael? My partner, Eddie, has loved cigars for years, and one day he was working in a cigar shop that we used to call "the office," and he and Michael ran into each other. They started just BS-ing, and next thing you know Michael says, "Why don't we work together? I offer on a couple of properties. If we can get a property possibly you'd let me list it." He put a little work forward. He didn't really want to represent us as buyers; that wasn't his business. His business was listing. He said, "Why don't I help you find a deal, and then you'll let me list it when the time is right?"

Fast forward to today. Michael has 13 of our listings, or maybe a couple less because I think we just sold some. He is a great team member. Where did we find him? At a cigar shop. You've got to get out there and talk about what you're doing. Be excited about what you're doing, because that excitement will raise other people's excitement. Get out there and just network. Go have a cup of coffee while you work for a little bit and see if you possibly get into a conversation. I've gotten into conversation after conversation in a coffee shop.

Where someone has overheard one of my phone calls, I've overheard someone else's phone call. I've heard a conversation; they've heard my conversation. They say, "Hey, I'm a realtor," "Hey, I'm a contractor," "Hey I'm a loan broker." Or possibly, "Hey, I hear you're a realtor. We're looking for deals; do you have any listings that I might like?" I introduce myself. I say hello; I just make that simple introduction. Networking is the number one way to build your team.

Let's talk about a couple of other people who are on

our team. What about accountants and lawyers? They may be some more of the professional team that you might want or need. We have not yet needed a lawyer, but we sure wanted one on our team in case that day ever came. So we went out and found one. We needed an accountant. Where would you guess we found those?

I'm not going to trust my livelihood to a lawyer I don't know and that no one's ever referred. I'm not going to trust my livelihood to an accountant no one knows and that no one's ever referred. I want referrals when it comes to those team members. In this type of industry, when it comes to law, to book keeping, to accounting, to IRS, I want someone I know is good, so I want referrals.

What about your social media? What about your website? What about that area of your business? I've coached hundreds if not thousands of students, and a lot of students really want a professional look before they get started as a real estate investor. They say, "There needs to be some legitimacy behind my company," and I absolutely understand where they're coming from.

Where do you find a web guy? Yes, referrals, absolutely. Web guys, social media guys, maybe even assistants, personal assistants or an assistant for your company. Where can you find them? How about down at your local college, and give them an internship with your company. When I was in college, and I'm sure you can all relate, you were looking to build your resume. You wanted to have something built so that when you got out of college you could find that right job and say, "I already have experience with all of this."

There is nothing worse than getting out of college having no experience and saying, "I can't get a job because I've got no experience, but how can I get experience if I can't get a job?" Throughout college I wanted to get that. When people would post about internships, paid or unpaid, I would reply to them if they dealt with the field I was interested in.

Right now, and I say this over and over again, you see that every television station has a real estate investing show on it. It's everywhere. The excitement about real estate investing is at an all-time high. If you're able, go down to your local college and post an internship. Go out there and offer up an internship, and you can find people to create a website. Most likely you're going to have to pay for that, but you may not have to pay top dollar. You may be able to find a tech person down at the college or a computer science major and simply offer him a couple hundred dollars to build up your website.

The same thing is true with your social media. Get your social media going. Get it connected with your website. Get it connected with your marketing. You could give that to your assistant. Maybe you just need an assistant for a couple of hours a day to answer the phone, to reply to certain emails, to send out some mailers, or whatever it may be. Where do you find them? What about college? And what about community service–type places or a non-profit? There are a lot of different areas. People want experience in this world. Look into those types of places to find someone who will do these activities for you. Those just a couple of suggestions on where to find them.

Realtors are a dime a dozen, right? But you've got to find a good realtor. Where would you find realtors? Besides just looking on the MLS or online, why don't you go to your title companies? They're probably going to give you a pretty good referral. They're going to know the real estate agent who's doing deals, who's successful, who's knowledgeable. It doesn't really matter which title company it is; go down there and see if you can get a referral or two.

Here's one of the things that a lot of people forget. There's a whole industry around virtual assistants, VAs. Maybe they're not team members that you can have a team meeting with in your office, but VAs are crucial when it comes to smaller tasks that you want done. Stuff like importing a list of buyers you built and dealing with the marketing of that. For us, we're writing books and doing podcasts, and we need art development and a lot of these smaller things. A virtual assistant would be less expensive than hiring a full-time person to do them.

Elance is a great company for finding virtual assistants. Go to Elance and figure out exactly what you need, and they will do it for $3, $4, $5 an hour. The project could be simply putting together your buyers' list or putting together some artwork for your website; you name it and they'll do it.

Another website a lot of people don't know about is Fiverr.com. Fiverr will do the same thing a virtual assistant would do. For us, transcribing books, giving a recording to them and saying, "Transcribe this into a book" has allowed us not to have to do it. You can get anything done on Fiverr, I don't care what you're trying to do, as long as it can be done remotely. It's not a team member whose hand you can physically shake and whom you can have a weekly meeting with, but still, you can continually go back to that same person on Fiverr or that same virtual assistant and have them continue to work on your projects.

If you are going to build a team, the most important part is making sure they have the systems in place to be efficient. There is nothing more frustrating than bringing a team member on and two or three months later turning around to check the results and finding that there are no results or they're not adequate, or you bring on a contractor and he's way over budget on a deal. There is nothing more frustrating than bringing on a team member who then doesn't give you results.

You can't point at them. You've got to point at yourself. Remember, this podcast is built for you to systemize your business so that you can literally be in Europe, or maybe you're coming to America, but either way you want to build a system for your business so that your team knows exactly what to do, how to do it, and what you're expecting in order to give you the results you want.

If you take nothing else away from this book, take this: provide the team with the system to do their job correctly. One of the best ways that Eddie and I give them a system is to simply record it on our computer. So if we're teaching a real estate agent how we analyze deals, we analyze it on our computer, record both the screen and what we're saying, and give it to them. There should be no questions after that. They have a 10- or 15-minute video on exactly how we analyze deals and what we're looking for, and there should be nothing to keep them from going and getting those deals. Record yourself, whether it's your voice or the screen or both; that way you have that system.

With our project manager, we have a workflow. One day we took the time to physically go through the day as if we were the project manager. We created a simple workflow on a document that said, "You need to fulfill these things on each and every rehab; here they are. When we buy a home, you go change the locks. Next day turn on the utilities; give us power and water. Next day make sure that the contractors are out there starting their rehab bid process. Next day, so on and so on and so on. Two days later, review all rehab bids by the multiple contractors. Next day, pick it and get them started. Finalize the draw request, activate the insurance, and so on and so on."

We now have a document that gives them the workflow that they can't mess up. If they mess up, now I can say, "You forgot this." I've given them everything they need to have a system for doing their job correctly. My expectation is that as long as they do everything on this workflow, we're going to get the result we want. If they don't do it, the next key is to get rid of them, whether it's a real estate agent, loan broker, contractor, someone you hired on Fiverr, some virtual assistant, your social media guy, or your website guy. If they're not producing the results you want, you need to get rid of them. Don't keep them on the team just because you're nice.

I can't tell you the number of meetings Eddie and I have had to walk into where we've had to basically say, "Get the job done or we're done with you. You're no longer working with us," or simply "We've given you plenty of shots, we're no longer working with you." We've had countless meetings, because not every realtor wants to work as hard as you want them to. Not every contractor can do the rehab within the budget they said they could. Not every web guy can budget the website. Not every selling realtor can negotiate the contracts the way you want them to. Not every project manager can manage your project the way you want them to.

You keep on with finding the right team members. Don't be afraid to shed the fat. If you feel that your business can be more efficient without a certain individual, let them go, but replace them because you don't want to be doing it yourself. That's the whole point: don't do it yourself. That's not what we're trying to teach you. We're trying to teach you how to utilize others so that you can be out and about.

You have to realize that if someone is not hitting the goals, you can either look at them or look at yourself. The only reason you would say, "Maybe this is my fault" is if you didn't give them the systems in the first place to do their job effectively and efficiently.

The next thing you can look at is, "All right, team member, all right, real estate agent, how do I incentivize you to do a better job? Okay, project manager, how do I incentivize you to do a better job?" It's pretty easy for realtors: give them more business. Maybe if they go out there and get you your deal, meaning they write an offer on your behalf, then maybe you also give them the listing on the back end. Maybe if they're your listing agent, instead of giving them 3 percent or 2 percent, if they bring the buyer you give them 4 percent.

The easiest way to build loyalty with your team or incentivize your team member is simply to keep giving them business and make sure you pay on time. I can tell you that if you don't pay on time people aren't very happy. They don't stay with you very long. We've made it a point to always pay on time, but some people you need to incentivize. With our project manager, we'll give a bonus if he can get the job completed. We just give him a $500 American Express card for doing such a great job over the last two or three deals.

He's been killing it. He's keeping the general contractor on budget. He's making sure the workflow works. He's doing a lot of work. We incentivize him by saying, "Here's $500 on an American Express card. Go have a good night, have a good weekend. Take your girl somewhere. Here's an incentive." He's going to come back from that weekend relaxed a little bit, maybe he's bought himself a new pair of shoes or whatever. Remember that you need to incentivize your team to do well, to be proactive and possibly handle things without having to come and ask you.

People need direction and want direction. That is why you build that workflow. You can build a workflow in a system for every one of your team members. As entrepreneurs, you're probably out there laughing, saying, "You're right. A lot of these people keep coming back to me and asking me questions about this, that, and the other," and that's just because you need to give them the direction, the system to do their job. You need to give them a manual so they don't have to ask you a bunch of questions and so they can do their job efficiently. Then instead of doing one property, you can do two or three properties.

Building your team is fun, but do it correctly. We're constantly building a team. We just brought on another real estate agent. He is an awesome buying agent, meaning he represents us as a buying agent for us. I think over the last two or three weeks we've closed two deals with him. He works hard. He understands what we want because Eddie had a video about how we analyze deals, where we want to buy, what we're looking at, and how we run the comps. He gets it. He doesn't need to ask us any more questions; he just goes. That's what you want from your team member.

That's how you build a successful team. Replace the people until you find the right ones. Don't just keep them on the team because you're nice and you don't know how to let them go. That's not going to create a happy atmosphere for you. You're not going to get the results that you want, they're not going to get the results that they want, and it's just not a good way to do business. Cut the fat; run lean and mean with the people who do their job well.

Building your team is not going to happen overnight. It takes time. If you're a rookie real estate investor, maybe you need to build the whole team. Maybe you need to find a title agent, a loan broker. Maybe you need a real estate agent, a contractor, accountants, lawyers, web guys, whatever it may be. Maybe you're an experienced veteran investor and you're killing it doing 50, 100 deals a year; maybe you just need one or two people. Today you got the advice to find that individual, and as you probably know, it's not an overnight thing. You have to remain consistent because not everyone is willing to put in the work, so you have to put in the work to find that right person.

The key is networking. Ask for referrals. Ask if people know of anyone. That's how you're going to find the majority of the good people, because someone's used their services before. Ask around. Don't be afraid to ask, and don't be afraid to create the system for what you need and give it to them. Put it on their table by saying, "This is exactly what your job entails. This is exactly how you do it and these are the results I'm looking for."

It's a fun thing, and when you build your team they start to become family. You start to enjoy them and you start to have holiday parties together and they become your family. You want to create a close-knit team, people you can consider family, and you run lean and mean. You don't need this huge organization.

Deal Analysis

This chapter is about deal analysis. How do you analyze deals in today's market and what do youdo with them? Primarily I'm going to be talking about analyzing deals so that it makes sense for your business, because not all of our real estate investing businesses are the same. My business, Phoenix Wealth Builders, really revolves around fixing and flipping. We're developing deals out in Meza, Arizona, and that's a great addition to what we've already been doing. I love it; there's always something new to do or learn and contracts to sign.

It's a lot more people and a lot more zeros, but there are many similarities between being a real estate developer and a fix-and-flip investor. We're able to use a lot of the same systems that we've built over time in our fix-and-flip business and apply them in the development world, but that's just part of it. For some, you want to buy property to hold. You buy it, fix a little bit, and make it rent ready. For others, you want to buy it and just sell it without putting any money into it. It's all about how you analyze the deal, so I'm going to go over how to analyze deals and how to fit that into your business.

First I want to tell you a quick story. It happened while we were at an auction buying a bunch of homes in 2011, and for whatever reason it was my day to analyze the deals and to be at auction. We had our list; we get a list every single morning about the deals that are going to be at auction. We whittle that down to the deals we like, analyze them, and have our highest bid planned.

They give us a starting bid and we figure out what our highest bid will be and hope to get it. We did very, very well, but there was one time—and it happens to all of us—that I didn't pay close enough attention to detail. And that's really what I'm going to hit home here right now: you've got to pay close attention to detail when you're analyzing deals.

It was my day and we started off pretty well. We got a deal that I felt pretty good about. A little bit later in the day we got another deal, and then this third deal came up and we were looking pretty good, and the starting bid was $36,000 and some change. So I started our bid there and I had the highest and best amount I was willing to go. We got the call that our opening bid was looking like we might get the deal.

I was on the phone with my guy down at the county courthouse steps and he was saying no one else was bidding and we were the only bid in there, and I was excited. It was close to the end of the day, so I was figuring maybe everyone already blew their money for the day; maybe this was the reason we were getting the deals. It was in the historic district of Phoenix and it would be the steal of the day if I could get it for this opening bid. We won and I was thrilled. We got three awesome homes; two of them were out in Meza and one of them was here in the historic district, all great areas to buy fix-and-flip properties. I was stoked.

We went to visit the home after we bought it, and it turned out this home was built in the 1930s. Arizona is not a very old state. This must have been one of the first homes ever built here in Phoenix. It could have been the first home ever built here; that's the condition it was in. It had a makeshift upstairs built with plywood. You could push the exterior wall of the house and the whole wall would literally shake. It was crazy.

Immediately I said, "Oh, no." Now every other home around there had been already brought to code and rehabbed to a certain extent or was built in a more recent year, and this home happened to be the one home on the block built in the 1930s. I swear I think this was the first home built in Arizona or at least in Phoenix. We had to figure out what to do.

We ended up actually selling it to a builder who had a much better understanding of what was going to need be done to this home because it was basically a teardown, and at that time we never built from the ground up. We sold it to a builder and walked away. We didn't take a loss; we really just broke even. I think we sold it for $39,000 or something, which would cover our cost of money and the fee we paid to buy it at auction.

We got out of that deal clean, but the point is that you have to pay attention to detail, because I had that intention in front of me when going through our list. I was really frustrated with myself because I didn't do anything wrong except that I just didn't pay attention to the detail of the home. The square footage was right, the area was right, and the price was right, but it was too old. We didn't want to buy a home built in the 1930s.

To this day we still don't want to. We don't really want to buy anything older than the 1960s. If we have to and it's in the right area, 1950s will work, but you need to pay attention to detail. Obviously one of the things you really want to pay attention to is the year it was built. Know when it was built and then know for that surrounding area what else has been built and what is the average year it was built.

The square footage of the property itself as well as the square footage of the lot: we've made a lot of money buying what might not be the sexiest home but the lot could be divided in two or even three. The lot would be huge, so that would give us room. Maybe the home itself didn't make a lot of money. Maybe we'd break even or maybe we'd make a couple of dollars, five or ten grand, but then we were able to sell the second lot for $30,000 or $40,000 for just the lot. You've got to pay attention to the lot size as well. A lot of investors forget about that; they forget about the creativity of buying a home that looks like you could only break even or make a dollar or two but then has an extra lot you can sell off.

You want to know how many beds and bath it is. It could be a huge house but still could just be two bedrooms, two baths. That is very common here in Arizona. If you're a fix-and-flip investor and you're really focusing on 3-2 and above, make sure you're looking at the bed and bath combo and whether you may need to add square footage. That's the first thing when you're analyzing a deal.

Figure out what subdivision it's in.

Start looking and coming, and when you're running your analysis look at that specific subdivision and the builders in it. What is being sold? What has been sold? What is pending? What is for sale and for what price? Pay attention to detail. We learned our lesson; actually I learned my lesson. This was years ago, and trust me, I'll never make that mistake again and I know Eddie won't either. He learned from my mistake. He's a smart guy.

When analyzing a deal, whether you're getting it from the MLS, a wholesaler, or the auction list , no matter where you're getting the deal, you can't rely solely on the numbers. A lot of times—let's just use the same example as the auction—some of the numbers look really good and it looks like you could buy this for $100,000 and like all the comps are selling for about

$215,000 to $225,000. Right away you might think, "I want this deal, absolutely, all day long," but you can't just run it by the numbers. You need to have an estimate in your head of what the rehab cost will be.

I'm going to bring up a couple of points here about holding cost and averages and paying for your insurance, your cost of money, your cost of sale (meaning commissions), and any type of concessions you're going to give; all that gets built into those numbers. What we will typically do is take 10 percent of what we're selling it at, and that's our cost. We reduce it by 10 percent immediately.

If we're going to sell it for $200,000, we need to reduce it by $20,000. If we buy it, we know right away that if we sell it at $200,000, the real number is going to be $180,000 because we're going to pay 6 percent commission, title insurance concessions, and so forth. Just because the numbers look good on a piece of paper, just because a wholesaler says, "The comps are this; you could buy it at this and make $100,000," that's not necessarily the case.

I mentioned the subject of a wholesaler or maybe a real estate agent who sends you a deal. The number one rule we live by here at Phoenix Wealth Builders is to never allow a wholesaler or a real estate agent to tell us what that home is worth. Never do we rely on their comps, because at the end of the day you have to remember that they're in it to make money also. A wholesaler wants to paint a beautiful picture of the value of this home and what it's going to be worth and how much spread is going to be in there so that you buy it so they make their wholesale fee.

Same thing with the real estate agent; they're going to paint a beautiful picture of the home, what you can buy it for, what you can sell it at, and how much you're going to make because they work off commission. Always remember that rule when analyzing a deal. Whether you get it from a wholesaler or a real estate agent, make sure you do your own analysis so you have the numbers you're really going to make on that deal. Never ever trust someone else to tell you what that home is worth.

The next thing I want to cover is super important, because the philosophy is that you make money when you buy the home. Your deal analysis is incredibly crucial. I mentioned briefly how you need to have an estimated rehab in your head when you're reviewing a deal. Let's say you're a rookie investor: how are you going to know?

So you're a rookie investor. You have no idea what these rehabs are. You've never done a rehab. What I suggest is that you first go figure out what the retail cost of materials are. Go to Lowe's or Home Depot and figure out what it costs for carpet per square foot, what it costs for tile per square foot. What is hardwood cost per square foot? What is paint cost per square foot? What is cabinet cost? What is granite cost per square foot? Formica cost per square foot?

Find out retail cost of the materials. Then you might need to do a little research and interview; buy a contractor some coffee and simply ask him what it would cost him per hour to do a rehab. The reason you want to do that as a rookie investor, or an investor who doesn't quite have the systems down yet to just be able to estimate a rehab bid, is to know how much a certain square foot house will cost and how quickly you can get it done.

You want to know how much per hour you're going to be paying the contractors. The hope is that the contractors are going to get you a deal on the materials. You need to know the retail first so that when the contractors say, "My bid is this. You're paying X for tile, Y for carpet, Z for the paint," you can compare that to the retail cost. Now you know whether you're paying retail or not.

For us out here in Phoenix, we know that if we're going to buy a 1500-square-foot home, a traditional 3-2, the rehab bid for the most part will come in around $30,000 to $35,000, give or take 10 percent. We have a 10 percent margin going either way. For $30,000, it could be closer to $35,000 or it could be closer to

$25,000. We know that primarily because of our experience. We've been doing this long enough.

Here's the thing: I spoke about how you never want to stop finding material, finding the better deal so you can save some money on your rehab. If you're an experienced investor, you'll have a pretty good idea of what these homes are going to cost. You know what it costs per square foot for all these materials and you really know what labor costs at this point. You need to have an estimated rehab and you also need to have a little bit of slush in that estimate so that you can have a little "Oh man money," as I like to call it—that's a nice way of saying it—but "Oh man, I didn't think about this" or "Oh man, I didn't know we're going to have to handle this part."

Because of that, you need to figure out what about that house is important that you're going to need to add value to or fix. For example, pools are great for here in Phoenix. A pool is a great thing to have for a home, but it could add possibly $5,000 to $10,000 to your budget depending on what you need to do to it, what kind of condition it's in. Roofs are another one; don't forget about having a roof in the budget. If the roof looks okay, that's fine, but nowadays buyers and lenders are so strict about what they're willing to accept that you need to budget a little bit of money for patching a roof or repairing part of a roof and getting it signed off by a roofing contractor.

If you have a carport or a garage, are you going to build that carport into a garage? Out here in Phoenix, a large percentage of homes have carports. When we see a home has a carport, we maybe budget for a garage. You need to have a little bit of that extra money in there to see if you can bring up the value of that home, whether it's a garage, a carport, a roof, or an air-conditioning unit. That's another big issue out here in Phoenix. A lot of you are in Pittsburgh or New York or Chicago and air-conditioning units might not be the big-ticket item, but out here it's over 100 degrees half the year. These things are important.

The next thing is I never suggest buying a house without stepping foot in it. And if you don't step foot in it, make sure someone you know does. We don't buy a home from a wholesaler unless I, Eddie, our project manager, one of our real estate agents, or the wholesaler himself can give us a detailed picture album showing the home. Really, we want to step into that home; we want to know exactly what we need to do for that home.

Again, we have a pretty good idea of square footage and what's actually going to be entailed there, but still we really suggest getting someone into that home, someone you trust, someone who is not going to be making a dollar when you buy it. That's our huge suggestion: make sure you see it. The reason is that you might be able to have a different set of glasses on.

You'll hear it a lot from me, but change the viewpoint of the glasses. Wholesaler, real estate agent, they may give you one set picture of that home, but you might walk in there and say, "You know what, we could probably add a bathroom, add a bedroom, increase the value by this, and get it sold for this much more." That is huge when you're analyzing a deal.

Being able to take a deal that looks like you could sell it for $200,000 as is after a rehab and then adding a bedroom to that home for, let's say, $5,000, but then you can get an extra $15,000 to $20,000 out of your resell price—that's how you analyze a deal, and you would not have known that without stepping inside that home. You want to be able to be creative when you're analyzing a deal.

We were recently looking at a 2-1. I'll tell you now, we don't buy two bedroom, one bath, but it's in a good area. We're taking a harder look at possibly making it a 3-2, adding two bathrooms or maybe one bathroom and a bedroom. Add two rooms to that house, add the square footage, get it permitted, and we might have a better deal. Most people would simply just let that deal fly by. "I don't buy 2-1, that's not my ballpark. That's not my sweet spot. I'm going to let it go."

Put on a different set of glasses, get into that home, and see if you can create the value. Add a pool, add square footage. That is how you can create some really good spreads in your fix-and-flip model—adding square footage. You might be able to walk into a place that is a dump and say, "You know what, it's going to be cheaper for me to tear this down and rebuild it from scratch. I'll make more money with everything brand-new because all these other comps are a half-mile away or brand-new subdivisions." You might be able to look at it with a certain set of eyes. Get your feet in that building or those of your project manager or someone you trust and who is not going to make money based on what they're telling you the home is worth.

Not to mention, you want to know what you're dealing with. I do not suggest buying a home you've never seen. Get out there and see it. If you're an experienced investor and you say, "I've been doing this now for five, 10, 15 years; I know exactly what a 2000-square-foot home is going to cost. I know what it is if it's built in the 1980s. I know all of that," okay, fine, I can respect that. When you have the experience, that's fine, but I still strongly suggest it, because you may make a huge mistake in that you know certain things but maybe you're not seeing the value you can add. I really suggest everyone get out there.

Lastly, I want to talk about exit strategy and then ultimately, when you're analyzing a deal, who you are selling it to. I'm a fix-and-flipper, so I want to fix it to the best of my ability. I don't want to hold any cost; I don't want to half-ass it; I want to get this thing pimped out. This thing's got to be shining. I'm going to spend the money to get it that way, but that's because I want to find the retail buyer. I want the family who's looking to upgrade or downgrade or buy a second home or whatever it may be. That's my exit strategy.

Here is the next point. I have a rental model strategy in which we traditionally stay in a price point where, in a worst-case scenario, should the economy fall apart again, these homes would be good rentals. They're not always going to be 10 percent, 12 percent, 15 percent rentals in a bad pinch, but we'll still get a good rental where we're either offsetting our cost of money or maybe making a little bit of money.

My exit strategy is 100 percent to retail that home, but when you're analyzing deals you need multiple exit strategies. What if scenarios happen? They just happen. It's real estate. You can plan, plan, plan but "what if" does happen. What if the economy crashes again? I don't want to be holding the bag with homes that are a million-plus. What happens then? You're going to get foreclosed on and everything else because the home dropped in value to a point where no one's going to buy it. We buy homes typically in a price point that could be turned into rentals.

Being in the position we're in, we do take on some of the bigger deals at higher price points, but for the most part we stay in a price point that will traditionally be a great rental in great areas.

You need to know your exit strategy. What if you're more of a buy-and-hold, meaning you're just going to be throwing on some paint, making sure the home is a good rental, and updating some stuff but you're not going to be dumping $40,000 or $35,000 in the rehab, you're going to be dumping $5,000 or $10,000 in carpet and paint?

That's your exit strategy. You get to analyze a deal in a certain way. You would probably buy a deal that maybe I wouldn't because you're not going to try to get top dollar. You don't need to spend $35,000 for your rehab. Know that when you're analyzing deals you have to understand your exit strategies. Who are you selling to? Are you going to buy a home intending to sell to a buy-and-hold investor, or are you going to buy a home intending to sell top dollar? Say you're going to dump a bunch of money into rehab and you want to sell for top dollar. I can tell you there are plenty of times that we'll analyze deals and it will be close, but it's just too thin. We don't want to do a deal for less than $10,000. We just don't want to do it.

I understand the price point here in Arizona, and there are thousands of you on the East Coast and in California who crack up when you hear you can buy an 1800-square-foot home for $150,000 out here built in the 1990s. You think it's the funniest thing ever because you're buying that same home for $500,000, $600,000, $700,000. I get it. That's why we're investors out here, but you need to have those types of exit strategies.

We stay at a certain price point because of that. We want to know that we have two different ways of selling it if something bad happens. This is crucial, and there are times where it's too thin. It would absolutely make sense for me to take a property and just go find a rental buyer for it, an investor who wants it as a rental, because it works all day long for that. So many times we're analyzing deals and it's just too thin. We're $2,000, $4,000, $5,000 off. We won't take the risk because it puts us under that $10,000 price point.

It doesn't make sense for us to do a deal for less than $10,000. Our price point is so low that we can do deals at $100,000 and we get $10,000 back. We basically run at a 10 percent model. If we're going to invest $100,000, we want to make $10,000. If we're going to invest $200,000, we want to make $20,000. If we're going to invest $300,000, we want to make $30,000. Above the $300,000 point, that's where it gets a little iffy. That's a little shaky for us, because no longer is it a 10 percent model. If we're going to dump $400,000, $500,000 into a fix-and-flip, we want to be making substantial money. We want to be getting close to a six-figure return, because there is not a lot of exit strategy when you get to that point.

When you're analyzing deals, for those of you who are in California or on the East Coast or in an area where you can't buy $100,000 homes and all you have are $500,000, $600,000, $700,000, $800,000 homes, there would be no way I would do that deal if I couldn't see six figures in it. No chance, because you don't have the same exit strategies that we have here in Phoenix. That's another reason we started investing in Phoenix. We do have multiple exit strategies, not to mention it's the fifth largest city in the nation with a ton of professional sports teams and a ton of added value to the city and it's sprawling and very wide.

You are probably laughing when you read about a $100,000 deal. I understand, but if I'm doing a deal for above $400,000, $500,000 here in Phoenix or elsewhere, I probably won't do it unless I'm going to get a six-figure return on it. There aren't the exit strategies. Make sure you know what you're doing and you know the numbers going in. if you're going to buy something high, make sure there are enough numbers in there.

Rehab Management

This is an important topic and one you need to understand. This is actually a subject I'm very passionate about; I enjoy our rehab business arguably the most out of all of them. You can definitely call managing rehabs one of my passions.

Hopefully I'm able to throw some tidbits out there that give some insight not only into our business model but will really help either start, grow, or expand on your fix-and-flip rehab business. I will stress that this is a moment in time. Our project manager that we have in place, our property runners, our general contractors, and the systems that we've created to be able to manage multiple rehabs in a volume market did not happen overnight, and when I say it's a moment in time, what that means is that it's constantly growing and changing and adapting.

I want to preface this by saying that we're constantly trying to tweak our model and adapt it and make it better. It may work better in some markets, than others, but with many of the core concepts of how we manage our rehabs, you'll be able to apply them in most all markets. I'm a big systems guy, so I'm really big on seeing something that works, making it leaner and meaner and systemizing it. I like automating things, systemizing things, and delegating.

With that said, I'll jump right into our structure. Eddie and I are in Phoenix, and we started at wholesaling but quickly transitioned to fix-and-flip. Our business is heavily based on volume now. We are in a lower price point market compared to where we're from in the San Francisco Bay area. With the private money we've raised and by leveraging with hard money, we've built a rehab business based on volume.

Our goal was to create a system and delegate to our project manager and property runners or to multiple project managers and general contractors to be able to do a minimum of three to five deals a month. We're really humming when we're doing eight to ten rehab flips every month. We capped out one month late last year in 2012 when we were doing, I think, 22 in one month. I believe that was the highest, and there were a lot of moving parts. There are a lot of cats to herd when you're doing 22 rehab deals simultaneously.

We found our sweet spot after months and years of doing this and it's right around eight or ten in the pipeline, which is great for us. If we're buying anywhere from three to five, constantly rehabbing three to five, and selling three to five, if there's that constant flow, that's where our sweet spot is.

As far as structure goes and what we've built to really help facilitate this seamlessly, if you can picture a mind map or a pyramid, Eddie and I are on top, and directly under us is our primary project manager. For simplification purposes, let's just work with one project manager. A question I often hear is "Where do you find a good project manager?" That really applies to any business. You want to make sure that it's the right personality, the right person. I have a strong belief that management skills are just as important as, if not more important than, a construction or real estate background.

I would prefer construction background and real estate experience, but I personally pay closer attention to their people management skills or their personality skills, because really what you're doing as a project manager is managing personalities. Yes, the knowledge of construction is important; yes, knowledge of real estate is important, but that can be learned. I can't stress management skills enough when you're looking for a project manager. It could be a real estate agent who wants to learn how to do fix-and-flips or it could be an intern from a local college who really wants to learn how to be an investor, and you can train them to look at the rehab process.

In my opinion, someone who has great, strong management skills and maybe even retail management experience, somebody who's good at dealing with people, is vital. Your project manager is going to see contractors, subcontractors, possibly investors sometimes at their highest and lowest points. When jobs are going great, everybody's happy andit's all cupcakes and rainbows, but if some things go wrong, and trust me, in the rehab business they do, that project manager has to really be able to manage those difficult personalities in tough times. With real estate agents, maybe retail managers, positions of that nature, look stronger at the people management skills. On a quick side note, we've gone through a couple of project managers in our six, seven, eight years of flipping real estate full time. Right now our project manager is actually Eddie's brother, and that came about through various things that all lined up.

We're very fortunate to have him and he's a great fit. He's a great people person; he manages people very well. He happens to also have a background in framing houses, cabinetry, finishing cabinets, and building cabinets, but that was years ago. More recently he was a top-level manager. He's very good with people, and that mixed experience has done very, very well within our real estate business.

Your project manager is really at the top of your pyramid, and right below him I would recommend putting a field supervisor or a property runner. That's somebody who can within an hour's notice run over to a property and take some quick pictures, maybe video sometimes, but primarily just pictures. We've created a very easy one-page checklist that basically just itemizes what we want the property runner to see inside and out of a house.

We simply ask the property runner to fill out the one-page checklist and take pictures of those subjects, and I'll get into that checklist in a little bit. But your project manager is above; then you have your property runner right below.

Underneath the project manager as well, if you're going to build a volume fix-and-flip business like we have, you want to have a minimum of at least one or two general contractors with their own set of subcontractors.

We currently have a good three or four different general contractors, and they can do about three rehab projects per contractor. If you can, picture this pyramid of your project manager at top and the three general contractors under him, and then under those general contractors are three or four rehab projects. If you've got three general contractors who can do three rehab projects at once, you can do nine simultaneous rehabs. It's very simple math, and I'll try to get to personalities of the general contractors as well and what to look for and what not to look for, but the main topic here is the actual workflow and the systemizing of the rehab management process from start to finish, just to outline how we do that business.

A lot of times people ask us how we travel so much. "How are you able to go back to the Bay Area, travel and see a football game up here, and then go visit family out in the East Coast?" Honestly, it's because of this system that we've set up in our fix-and-flip business and other systems in the other branches of our business. This is really I want to talk about, the workflow itself.

Let's say a property comes across my desk. I greenlight it as far as it makes sense. It fits our rehab model. We want to purchase it. We tell the seller that we're a green light; we're a go on the property. We'll get earnest money down to title and whatnot. Originally what we'll do is offer him properties with at least a three-day inspection period. However, we've explained to our project manager and property runners that within two or three hours of our call they've got to get down to the property and access it.

Starting from scratch and going down nine or ten bullet points, when I green-light a property for acquisition, we immediately reach out to our project manager with the address and provide some pertinent details about it. Obviously if this is a vacant property we'll give them the lockbox code or access information, and ideally the project manager will go down there to access the property. This is, again, before we've closed; we've given the green light to purchase it, but we're in something of an inspection period, if you will. A lot of times we'll buy a property sight unseen, but if we have an inspection period, we'll definitely get our own eyes on it as soon as we can.

So as soon as I green-light, I'll send a text or more often an email to a project manager and he'll shoot down there. Again it's just address and lockbox code. He'll get in there and do his initial inspection. He'll have a one-page checklist and fill that out if necessary. That checklist is broken down into a few categories—kitchen, bathrooms, living area, yards—and is mainly to say, "What's the general condition of the dry wall, the flooring, the counters, the cabinets?"

If the project manager can get in there and write a few notes on the kitchen like "Cabinet boxes can be salvaged; we'll just refinish the fronts," then from our standpoint in the rehab budget we know we can save a few thousand dollars. That's why putting your own eyes on it helps.

That's really what the checklist is, things that I didn't see on just the pictures from the MLS or that the wholesaler or seller sent me. Really having your own eyes on it helps, so that checklist will be filled out and pictures will be taken, often a video. We ask for a three-to five-minute video, which we call an initial walkthrough video, and we train our project manager to shoot it starting in the front yard, walking all the way through the house, showing all the bedrooms, bathrooms, living area, kitchen, backyard, everything, and even walk through some initial ideas for rehab.

That comes with time, with your project manager learning how you rehab houses and what you're looking for, but really it's us getting that video in front of us as if we were there ourselves.

Our project manager then locks the house back up and leaves.

As he leaves, he uploads the pictures to a Dropbox folder we have, which is just virtual cloud storage. It links to your smartphone or your iPad or whatever you use. If you're taking pictures with your iPhone, for example, you have a Dropbox app with which you can upload the photos right to our shared Dropbox folder. He labels it "123 Main Street initial pictures" and those will appear immediately in our Dropbox folder. For the video we have a private YouTube channel, so if he's shooting a video on his iPhone, he'll immediately upload it to our private YouTube channel and email us the link or notify us that it's up.

If you can imagine, we are still in our offices, taking meetings, travellng, at home, doing whatever we want to do, and electronically we have pictures and video popping up in our Dropbox and YouTube channel that we can access and look at. If we see any surprises we can go back to the seller and say, "Look, in our inspection period we found this, that, and the other thing." It can sometimes be a negotiating tool; it really gives us a good idea of what we're going to need in terms of rehab budget.

Once that happens and there are no surprises, we fund, we record, and now we own the home. We send the project manager back out to the home as soon as we fund and record. As soon as title sends us an email saying, "Congratulations. It's funded and recorded. You're now the owners," another email goes out to our property manager. They go to the property and immediately lock out secure or clean out secure. Sometimes they'll do an initial trash-out if it's light work, but mainly the purpose is to just change all the locks in the property as soon as we own the home.

After the locks are changed we'll hang our own combo lockbox, and at that point whatever general contractor is next in line for a job will meet our project manager at that lock change so they can start building a scope of work together. Our project manager will walk the general contractor through the vision of what we want to rehab such as knocking out a few walls, standard cabinet, standard paint, standard flooring. We use a lot of the same materials because, again, we are in a volume business; a lot of times some of the color choices and finishing are already decided.

It's more about making any sort of structural changes, internally knocking out walls here and there. Actually we recently bought a house that was a three bedroom, one bath but the garage itself was the third bedroom; it was a permitted conversion to a bedroom. Although it was permitted, it wasn't done very well, and we bought it as a 3-1 with no covered parking, and in this neighborhood we love covered parking for our resell.

What we did was we found some room in the back of the house without changing the actual exterior walls. We were able to reconvert the third bedroom into a two-car garage as it originally was, and we added a third bedroom on the back of the house, a storage room that we reformatted into a bedroom. And we added another half bath. We actually turned it into a 3-2 with a two-car garage, immediately adding value. That was all done after we got our initial video. When that video came through, we talked about it with our project manager and gave him the ideas based on the video alone. The project manager went down to change the locks and spoke with the general contractor about those ideas during the scope of work process.

Again, it's kind of a step two process when the locks are being changed. The ideal is to meet the general contractor, go over the scope of work, and really tell him what you want on that bid, and our general contractors understand that we like to have our line item rehab bids back to us within 48 hours. We understand that a lot of the general contractors need to get their particular subs in there, electrical subs and plumbing and whatnot, and we understand that can't be a few hours' turnaround; 48 hours is usually fair in our mind.

Forty-eight hours later we'll have a line item bid on our desk. In the meantime, our project managers are responsible for calling the utility companies and turning on power and water. One step we added is to have a signpost company called and they put the poster in front. We have a system similar to the way real estate agents put their for-sale signs out there with their picture and their phone number on them. We have a similar concept with our logo, and it says "Another Neighborhood Beautification by Phoenix Wealth Builders" with our website URL under our logo.

We've actually gotten quite a bit of buzz that way. People driving by our rehab projects want to know if someone is moving in, if they're doing a rehab project, and who it is? With our neighborhood beautification sign there with our website, a lot of people have checked out our website, signed in, gotten a free giveaway, and emailed us, and we've gotten some positive feedback from it. That is little bit of marketing and branding that we do in the rehab management process. Day one of demo, so to speak, our sign's already out there. Everybody knows who's doing the rehab.

So power and water is on, and our Phoenix Wealth Builders neighborhood beatification sign is out front. We have our video and we have our scope of work.

Forty-eight hours go by and we have our line item bid. When that bid comes in to our project manager, these contractors know that we know what the cost should be. There's really not too much wool being pulled over the eyes in our business these days, because we've been doing it for a while and they're familiar with us and vice versa.

There's not a lot of tweaking and changing. We'll sometimes ask why this is changed from last time and why are these numbers different from this number and we'll beat them up, so to speak, when applicable, but other than that we'll green-light a bid right away if it all makes sense. If it's within budget, we sign a contract with our general contractor basically just laying out the rehab timeline and the draw structure, which I can touch on.

That is definitely part of the process, so I do want to say that when we green-light a bid, our typical rehab takes four weeks. The way we've set up our rehabs, we do a very simple one-page contract that says, "We approve X amount of dollars." We'll give four weeks; the approved budget is $30,000. Draw number one will be 50 percent of the rehab budget, so in this example it will be $15,000 for draw number one and that's due on day one of demo.

A lot of people ask me why so much? Why such a heavy draw up front? The major reasons are that with all the details a lot of the ordering happens up front. The cabinets especially and sometimes the flooring have to be ordered early in the rehab process so they don't hold you up in the back end.

Cabinets are one of the things that take the longest, depending on your market and your suppliers. It ebbs and flows depending on the distributors and the manufacturers, but cabinets and floorings are usually what take the longest, sometimes countertops. But again we do the larger draws up front so materials can be ordered and crews can start working.

The second draw will be 20 percent and that's due two weeks in, which is the halfway point depending on the progress. I'm going to touch later on how we know about progress; it obviously involves our project manager because they're constantly checking in on our rehab projects, but assuming that the progress is what we expect, draw number two happens at the two-week mark or the halfway mark. Again that is 20 percent.

Actually we flip-flop it; sometimes it's 30 percent. And then the last draw is released only at final walkthrough approval. I'll cover that last process and what the final walkthrough looks like, but just to finish speaking about what our contract looks like with the general contractor, it's a three-draw structure over a four-week period. Fifty percent is the first draw, 30 percent is the second draw, and 20 percent is the third draw. That's at final walkthrough and approval.

The general contractor understands from the beginning that they have four weeks. They know how much they're getting paid because we'll break down the percentage and what it equals in the draw structure. We'll give them the exact dates that the draws will hit their bank account, and they know that if it goes past the four-week mark, we charge $100 per day. Every day it goes past the contracted deadline, it's $100 a day taken off that final draw until the rehab is complete.

Some people play with a much larger per diem, some do less, but it is definitely incentive. Many times we'll not only incentivize with the stick but we'll incentivize with a carrot, and if they get done ahead of time, under that four-week mark, we'll sometimes offer a bonus structure as well.

After we get the line item bid, we approve it. We draw up that quick one-page contract I just outlined for you and they start demo. As soon as demo starts and day one of rehab starts and that clock's ticking, our project manager is responsible for taking a three- to five-minute rehab video update twice a week for each property. If 123 Main Street starts on a Monday, our project manager will go there probably on Tuesday or Wednesday and take a three- to five- minute progress report video, and at that point, two to three days in, it will show demo being complete and really starting to get into the guts of the home. He'll stop by again a few days later, maybe 1 Saturday or Sunday, and show the progress that has been made.

Keep in mind that as those videos are taken they get uploaded to our YouTube channel. We can be anywhere—vacationing, at home, at our office, making our highest and best use of time, building a business, growing a business, taking meetings, networking, spending more time with family and friends, doing what really matters—and we're still plugged into our business because we have automated and systemized and delegated to the key players in our business model.

Let's say you have five or 10 rehab projects going. That project manager is stopping in twice a week at every single property. A project manager can't be everywhere at once, but we have found in our market and with the properties that we buy, eight or 10 properties for one project manager is about their limit. On simple logistics, it's very difficult to be running all over town and taking initial videos and pictures, and that's why we've leveraged the project manager by using a property runner to help out as an assistant. They do those initial walkthroughs, those initial viewings and picture taking and checklist filling out.

Going back to the system, we have a meeting once a week on Wednesday mornings at 10 a.m. Our project manager will sit in on our company meeting, and we go through acquisitions, we go through rehab, we go through what's in our pipeline to sell, and we just go around and around with all the departments in our rehab business. So we're not only getting two videos a week per property, but we also have our project manager sitting in the office for an hour or two on Wednesday mornings telling us all the nitty-gritty details of what's going on.

The project manager's also required by Friday or Saturday to send a progress update on all the rehab. We get one long comprehensive email at the end of the work week on every single property: the address, the lockbox code, the most recent video link, what stage of rehab it's in, the completion date if that's changed, and any pertinent notes.

Our project manager, our property runner, and our general contractors have handled it all so far. Let's dive back into our example rehab before we can mark this up. Let's say it's on time. The general contractor says rehab is complete. Our project manager schedules a final walkthrough with our listing agent; the walkthrough happens with the project manager and the listing agent. The reason we want the project manager there is obvious. He's managed the entire project from the beginning; he's the main liaison between the general contractor and us. The project manager is very intimately involved with that rehab progress, so he'll be able to speak to the listing agent.

The reason we want the listing agent at the final walkthrough is because that's who's responsible for selling that house, putting it on the market, bringing a buyer, and selling it for top dollar, getting it unloaded and off our books sooner rather than later. We want the listing agent there because he looks at it from a buyer's perspective.

That process is really just a blue tape process. The final walkthrough is supposed to be 100 percent complete by the general contractor and the project manager's eye. If there's paint touchup or little things here or there, if anything pops up, they're just minor things that can be done very, very quickly within a couple of hours or so. We like to have the final clean done by the time we have a walkthrough.

Let's say everything goes well at the walkthrough. Our project manager and our listing agent will both let us know that it's fully approved and good to activate on the MLS, or good to sell. At that point we'll release the final and third rehab draw to the general contractor so they're all done and paid, and we have them sign a lien waiver basically saying, "In exchange for this last rehab payment or draw, I'm waiving all my rights to file a contractor's lien or mechanic's lien on this property." It's acknowledging that they're paid in full. It's a key component.

Now that the contractor's done you hopefully don't

have to see him back again, but that's kind of classroom world, so to speak; in the real world there's a process. When a buyer comes and they're in escrow, inspectors and appraisers come. More often than not there are little things that an inspector will find and they say, "No, this has to be tweaked or fixed or patched up this way in order for the bank to fund the buyer's loan." Sometimes you'll have to call that general contractor back when your buyer's in escrow to fix a few of those inspection items, but other than that, for all intents and purposes your general contractor's done at that point.

Now comes the sales process. The project manager scheduled that walkthrough and the listing agent met him there and did that walk. Immediately we shift focus from the project manager to the listing agent. As soon as that final walkthrough is done and approved, the listing agent is in charge of contacting the stager so they'll either lightly stage or fully stage our properties with furnishings, wall hangings, artwork, sometimes a fake LCD or flat screen in the room, bathroom towels; it really just gives it that lived-in feel.

The listing agent is also responsible for scheduling the professional photographer. We get the stager there, and as soon as the stager is done, we want the professional photographer to come in and take the nice pictures and video for our virtual tour. Those pictures take a day or so to come back, and once we get those professional photos back we can activate the MLS listing. As soon as we go live with the new listing, we have it staged with professional photos and it's listed active on the MLS.

At that point, that's what the listing agent is basically commissioned with.

Shifting focus back to the project manager, after that final walkthrough is done and they give us the green light to pay the final draw and get the lien waiver, the project manager switches our signs out front and it goes from the 'Phoenix Wealth Builders Neighborhood Beautification" sign to the listing agent's sign. It's literally just a swap of the sign out front.

Our project manager then cancels the utilities. They actually keep the utilities on for escrow a lot of times, especially in summer when they keep the AC on for showings, but those utilities usually get shut off at the end of the buyer's escrow. That is a couple more tasks just like the ones they initiated; the project manager initiated utilities in the front end and he will also discontinue the services after our buyer closes.

At this point, we're all done. The contractors are paid and gone. We have our staging furniture in; our pictures are done. It's activated on the MLS. We get an offer and we negotiate. Let's say we accept an offer; we typically enter a 30- to 45-day escrow. We don't usually have our appliances put in until the buyer's in escrow. That cuts down on the possibililty of theft; it gives people less reason to break in if you don't have nice stainless steel appliances there, so we usually install the stainless steel appliance package in escrow.

Escrow is moving; the inspection's being done; the appraisal's being done. If there's any inspection item that pops up, the project manager will notify our general contractor who did the rehab. They'll do those little tweaks and fixes to make everything good to close, and then once that is funded, our buyer closes and records. That's when our project manager shuts off utilities and we're good to go.

That's really the overall broad-stroke summarized version, kind of a snapshot from elevation of our rehab management process and our workflow. As you can see, it's heavily about automating, systemizing, and delegating so that we can be making our highest and best use of time, doing what we want to do, growing and expanding our business, and we still are plugged in and dialed in to our rehabs. We know exactly what's going on at all times.

If we've raised certain private money who wants to know, "Hey, how's the rehab going down at 123 Main Street that you used some of my private funds on?" we can immediately pull up the most recent video, send them a link, and say, "It's looking good. Here's a video we shot a couple days ago. Our team was just down there; looks like we're on schedule to finish on time." You can always be plugged in in this virtual electronic world that we're living in now with everything at your fingertips. We're able to stay plugged in wherever we are, and the reason I like this process so much is that I love what we do.

The fix-and-flip of the house is a win-win for everybody involved, but what really gets me going is that we can do this numerous times over and over and I'm not even going to the house. I never step foot at a house that we buy, rehab, and resell. I can tell you I don't even go down to the vast majority of houses we've done this year. I usually only end up going to our properties if I want to or if an investor is in town and wants to see some of our projects. We very rarely go to the properties ourselves now, and that's great. That's when you really know that you have built a business as supposed to just building a job, in my opinion. You own a business when you don't have to be down there and hands-on, yet you're still 100 percent plugged in.

Marketing For Sellers

There are a lot of different ways to market real estate right now in this economy. We're going to separate the topic into paid marketing and unpaid marketing. My business partner, Eddie, always says that there are really only two ways to get deals or buyers: network and marketing. You've got to do one of those two, and that's really how I break down marketing in general—you either pay for it or you don't. If you're not going to pay for it, then you're going to network. Let's start there.

Unpaid marketing for the most part is just getting yourself out there. I've talked time and time again about networking, but the reality is that it is super important in your real estate business and you need to be doing it. I've told you the stories of how when we first started I would sit and cold call real estate agents. I would line up meeting after meeting at Starbucks and network with these agents so that they would represent us on their listings. Cold calling is a way to set up your networking meetings; you can simply cold call real estate agents, title companies, loan brokers, hard money lenders, you name it, and be networking with these people depending on what you're looking for. In this economy in this real estate market we're looking for the deal.

Right now there's very little inventory, so that's really what everyone is focused on, where to find the deal. If you're going to be networking, who else has deals besides real estate agents, other investors, title companies, loan brokers, and hard money lenders? Listen, a lot of people don't even think about calling hard money lenders; they have to default on fix-and-flip investors at times because they haven't been paying their loans. Talk about a ninja way to find inventory: start networking with your hard money lenders to see if they have any homes they're going to have to take back that you could simply buy from them, take over the loan, whatever that may look like. But go out there and network by cold calling everyone in the industry that you can possibly connect with.

If you're going to the REIA meetings and the title company meetings anyway, continue to network with the people you meet there. If you're looking to build a buyers list, that's how you build it without paying for it. If you're looking to find deals, network with real estate agents, hard money lenders, loan brokers; those are people who are going to find you deals that aren't necessarily on the MLS.

This is all unpaid marketing. You're either going to spend money or you're going to spend time in your marketing. What I'm saying is these are ways to network so that you don't have to spend money.

Sometimes you can get away with what I would consider paid marketing but you're still doing it yourself, which helps you save money. That could be something like bandit signs. You can go out and get simple little white corrugated boards at Lowe's or Home Depot, 100 or 200 of them, and do them yourself rather than hiring someone to do them, right?

Again, you're spending one of two things, and maybe you're spending both, but to limit your spending of a lot of money you'll have to spend time. Even with paid marketing—which we'll talk about in a little bit because there's other unpaid marketing to go over—you can utilize bandit signs as a good way to limit expense, and even with your direct mailers, you can do it yourself instead of hiring someone or paying a company to do it.

You'll have to spend time networking, cold calling, and setting up meetings. Simply ask for referrals when you're in those one-on-one meetings. Referrals are huge portion of anyone's business in real estate, whether you're a real estate agent, loan broker, hard money lender, whoever. If you're an investor treat it the same way—ask for referrals. Let's say you get a really hot seller lead and you go to their home and are able to get them in contract, and you're looking to buy the home, rehab it, and flip it. Why wouldn't you ask, "Hey, do you have any friends or family looking to do the same thing? In the same situation you're in, do you know anyone else who could benefit from me buying their home?" Ask for that referral, because almost every time I ask for a referral, I get what I'm asking for. You'd be amazed what you can get just by asking.

Here's a little ninja tip I'll give you about unpaid marketing: YouTube. YouTube right now is the most ninja way for you to go out there and market for sellers, buyers, lenders, whatever you want to market for, because guess who owns YouTube? YouTube is owned by Google. If you go out there and produce high-quality YouTube videos with great content and you're able to SEO that video with the right title and the right subject and description, you will get ranked on Google and you can drive people from your YouTube video to a capture page. So if you're looking for sellers or buyers or lenders or whoever, utilize the power of YouTube, because it will rank you on Google. Then when someone types "quickest way to sell a home" or "more inventory in Phoenix, Arizona" or whatever they're looking for on Google, your YouTube video will be highly ranked within their search. Maybe they Google "lending on real estate" or "real estate investors in Phoenix," and there you are; there's your YouTube video.

That is my real gold nugget for this topic, because a lot of people don't know that Google owns YouTube and don't understand the power of YouTube videos in Google. It doesn't cost you anything to make a YouTube video. You just have to make it, get some SEO tips on what to make the subject and title, and throw it up there. And people who are looking for the same subject will find you because you'll be ranked in Google. Again, that is so important for you to understand. That is the golden nugget for this episode. Take notes and create YouTube videos. Don't worry about what you look like; you look like that every day. Create the video; get out there.

Let's move on to paid marketing. When we first started out, we didn't have a lot of money to pay for marketing. We did exactly what we're telling you to do; we did grassroots networking. Anyone I met I would ask for a referral. I went to all the networking meetings, all the title company meetings, and I would consistently try to network. And because of that we got our first two deals done, and then because we had our first two deals we continued to grow our network and eventually were able to get more realtors, more leads, and more buyers. And it was all through networking.

Once we created some income for ourselves, we started paying for our marketing. We started utilizing direct mail. Direct mail is my favorite way of marketing right now. Currently I know of three or four investors here in Phoenix who are spending anywhere from $10,000 to $40,000 a month on direct mail. Why? Because they're wholesalers looking to find deals, that's why, and they need to outmarket everyone else. If they want to keep a volume of 30 or 40 homes every single month, they need to find those off-market deals and they use direct mail. I also use direct mail. We don't spend $30,000 to

$40,000 a month, but we'll spend a good amount every month to keep a high volume of fix-and-flips going here at Phoenix Wealth Builders, and direct mail is our number one way.

If you don't have a lot of money, you can simply get a list of absentee owners, high-equity owners, free-and-clear owners, divorce situations, inheritance, probate, and so on. You can get that list. I have a database that gives me high-equity, free-and-clear, and absentee owners; I bought the database. I think I spend something like 91 cents per mailer, and the reason that may sound high is that it includes everything: postage, mailing, the copy on the mailer, the material, everything. It's a database, a one-stop shop, and we send it out and it's incredibly effective.

We just sent out 200 mailings, which is not a lot, and got two deals from those 200 mailings. Can you imagine how many more of those mailings we're going to send out? The copy is already written and everything is already set up; it's very, very effective. We love direct mail.

Direct mail is also another way that we find cash buyers or build our buyers list in general. We have a similar database that scrubs all the public records for cash-buying individuals and investors, and we add them to our database. We send out a mailer to those individuals or LLCs simply saying, "We saw that you bought a property for cash at 123 Main Street. We bought 1234 Main Street. Would you be interested? Give us a call or go to our website and give us your information." These databases scrub the public reports every two or three weeks so they have the most up-to-date information. We can look for zip code; it's good all the way across the country, so if we decided to start investing in Pittsburgh, Pennsylvania, we could still utilize this.

We love direct mail, but if you don't have the money to buy the database you're going to have to buy some sort of list, and if you don't have the money to hire someone to do the mailings for you, you're going to have to write the mailers. You'll have to stuff the envelopes and mail them. It will save you a lot of money. We choose not to go that route. We choose to go to the one-stop shop, but still the database is great and it is not very expensive.

Direct mail is our preferred way of marketing for buyers and sellers and lenders, you name it. We also send a mailer out for lenders, people who are giving private loans on real estate transactions. These are all public records; we're not doing anything that you can't do, but we ended up buying a database. That same database does exactly what I was explaining before, scrubs the public records and finds all private individuals who have put a deed of trust on a property here in Phoenix, and we mail to them saying, "I saw that you put a deed of trust on 1234 Main Street. I just bought 12345 Main Street. Why don't you give me a call so we can talk further about what you're looking to get back from your investment?" Direct mail is our number one avenue for everything—buyers, sellers, lenders. That is how we work it.

There are a lot of other avenues for marketing. What about a website? If you're able to create a good website and SEO it, you can drive a lot of traffic to yourself, whether you're looking for buyers, sellers, lenders, or whatever. If you know how to organically SEO your website, which means search engine optimization, I have a lot of investors who are very good at that. They get a lot of traffic to their website to build their buyers list and sellers list because that's what they SEO it for. It requires some time involvement and you'll have spend some money having someone to do that unless you know exactly how to do it, but websites are great ways to build your buyers or sellers list or even find lenders out there online.

What about pay-per-click advertising on Facebook, LinkedIn, or Google? Use pay-per-click to drive them to that same website. I've run pay-per-click advertising for a multitude of things. We coach hundreds if not thousands of students, or if it's an event we're putting on or a product we're an affiliate for, we will drive them to our website. We pay something like 25 cents per click, and then we cap how many people can click it and what we're willing to spend. They'll click 100 times a day and we'll say we're only willing to spend $100 a day on this pay-per-click advertising, but what the advertising does is drive them right into that website that we were just talking about, straight into that website for us to capture their information.

Newspapers are kind of a dead industry right now; they're still alive, but they're not utilized the same way they used to be. Pay-per-click ads on Google, Facebook, and LinkedIn are much more effective these days than newspaper advertisements. However, newspaper and magazine advertisements still work, but you need to figure out exactly what you're marketing for. Have a game plan. Where is that ad going to drive them? If you're looking for buyers or sellers, what is that ad going to say? "We buy ugly houses," "We close, quick cash"; whatever that advertisement says, you have to drive them back to that website so you can capture their information so you can speak to them. The newspaper or magazine ad needs to be very specific, and it can be very expensive, but you need to drive the reader back to the website that you already created.

Door hangers: I have a funny story. When I first started in real estate I was up in Northern California. I was working as a real estate agent, and I felt that using door hangers and actually going out there and hanging them myself would be the most efficient because I didn't have a whole lot of money, so I figured why pay for someone to send out these mailers? Why don't I just go and put them in the mailbox or put them on the door myself? That actually led to leads. People would be around; they'd just be getting home, in their driveway or mowing their lawn, and they'd ask me what I was doing, what I was giving this out for, and they would get engaged by me. Again, door hangers take a little bit of money to create, but if you do it yourself, you're only investing your time. You're investing something you have that you don't need to spend more money on, and you can go create those leads because you're out there engaging these individuals.

What about bandit signs? This is one of my favorites again. These work like crazy. You put bandit signs out there that say something like "Looking to sell your home? We close, quick cash" with your phone number, and you put them at hot intersections where you know there's going to be a lot of traffic. It absolutely works. As I mentioned, you can have someone do all of it from A to Z; they will write the sign for you and place the sign for you, all of it. That's going to be more expensive. In fact, I just did that a couple of weeks ago and I think I spent about $1,000 on 500 bandit signs to be placed. I paid for the materials, I paid for their time, and I paid for them to place them. It's a little bit more expensive. It probably would have only cost me about $500 total for 1,000 bandit signs if I was willing to just buy them, or even less than that if I was going to just buy the materials and write them myself. It is a paid way of marketing, but you can really limit how much you're paying and it absolutely works.

Radio is another one of my favorites. I love using radio. In fact, you guys are listening to me doing a podcast. This is a free podcast, but radio is more expensive. You'll have to pay for your air time. Radio has all different situations, peak hours and non-peak hours. When people are driving in their car it's considered peak hours, and non-peak hours would be dinnertime. What you'll pay and for how long is going to vary, but radio is very, very effective. Some of my friends who are in a different industry use radio and spend a lot of money on it, but the return on their investment is just incredible.

That's the last thing I want to bring up here: what your return on investment is going to be when you're actually paying for your advertising. That is what you have to look for and where you have to crunch the numbers. If you're spending $1,000 on direct mail and you want to get a 1 percent to 2 percent return on it, are you going to get a deal out of that? You have to work it backwards. The key to your marketing is to track what is working. No matter what you do, that will be the key to your marketing.

If you're planning to spend $1,000, how many leads are going to come in? And then out of those leads how many deals are you going to get? Now you know how many mailers you'll have to send out. You need to track it and see what rate of return you're going to get on your investment. You're investing in your company; that's what marketing is, and I highly suggest you go and crunch some numbers. If you're going to spend $500 or $1,000, how many deals can you get from that? How often are you spending it?

Marketing involves (A) tracking it and (B) being persistent. When we send mailers, we don't send one mailer to one person and that's it. If we choose 1,000 people to mail to, we don't mail those 1000 people one time; we hit them a minimum of three times. That's a minimum. Sometimes it's four or five times, but it's a minimum of three times; that way we feel that they've been hit. The standard in the real estate industry is three times, so we stick with that. Then we move on to another group of individuals whom we will also hit three times.

Now, if we were sending out 1,000 mailers at $1 apiece, that's $1,000. How often are you sending out those mailers? And then how many times are you sending them to the same people? You have to break that down. You need to know how many deals you're getting from those mailers. The same is true for radio advertisements, newspaper advertisements, pay-per-click advertisements, bandit signs, or any paid marketing. You need to look at the investment you're making, how many leads that brought you, and out of those leads how many deals you got. Then you're going to know how much you paid per lead. If I get two deals after spending $1,000, I paid $500 for each of those deals. That cost is part of that fix-and-flip deal I just got. I add the $500 into the cost of each of those deals. What's very important that not a lot of investors or marketers think about is how much you are paying per deal. You need to track that.

Let's say we do some pay-per-click ads, mailers or any of the direct ads, newspapers, bandit signs, or radio, and we get very little traction. Well, something's wrong, but you don't necessarily give up the first time. And I'm going to use mailers as an example because I love mailers: you send out 1,000 mailers and get one call. That's a horrible percentage, but you send them again to the same people because, again, remember, you've got to send them three times to the same people. If you don't have a lot of money and you're a rookie out there, don't send 1,000 mailers; send 200, 300, 400, 500, or whatever you can afford. You also need to look at your budget, because you plan to send it to the same people a minimum of three times. I would say send the mailer once every three weeks to the same people three times, meaning that after a little over two months, you're done mailing to those individuals. But you need to budget.

If you have $500 budgeted for marketing, you might only want to do $200 or 200 mailers at $1 apiece, or maybe you need to spend a little more time and write and send out your own mailers so you can save some

117

money so you can do a higher volume. But the key here, no matter what type of marketing you're doing, is to budget how much you have every single month to spend on marketing. Send it consistently, meaning if we're talking about direct mailers, send it three times. Run a pay-per-click ad for a consistent amount of time. Be in the newspaper more than once. Put out multiple bandit signs. Have a radio ad that runs multiple times. Have a website that's SEO'd. Put out hundreds of door hangers.

Frequency is huge. You have to be frequent when you are marketing and you have to be consistent. Once you are consistent and you're not getting the results you need, then maybe you need to redo your copy. Maybe what you're saying and how you're saying it is not resonating with these people. Redo your copy and resend it to them, whether it's a newspaper, a radio ad, a website, or whatever. Put different copy in there and give them a different message. If I'm focusing on people who want to sell ugly houses or sell fast, maybe I'm going after the wrong people in the way I'm saying it because maybe they want to sell but won't be able to close because they just inherited the property from their grandparents. They can't close fast; they have to be a little bit more patient. Rearrange what you're saying to them, what your message is.

Be consistent and then track your results, track your results, track your results. I can't say it enough, because if you're not getting the return you want, if you're not getting 1 to 2 percent and you're not getting your deals and you're not tracking them, you don't know what's working. Make sure you're tracking them. Make sure you know what's working and what's not working so you can change it for the next go-round, the next set of mailers, the next newspaper ad.

If you get a deal (or two or three or four) out of the marketing you did, make sure to attribute how much you spent in that marketing. If you had to do three or four mailers to get two deals and you spent $3,000 or $4,000 for those two deals, know that you ended up spending $2,000 on marketing per deal and put that into the cost of that deal. It's part of your cost as marketing cost.

What's Happening In The Current Market?

I get emails, text messages, and phone calls from hundreds of our students asking what's going on in today's market. They say, "What's going on with one of our properties? Why hasn't it been on the market? Why aren't we getting offers?" This chapter revolves around what is happening in today's market, because if you're out there and you're an experienced investor, you know there's been a big change and a big swoop into our market. Today we'll talk about what's going on in the market.

So what is going on? What's happened? Are there many deals right now? Are homes flying off the shelves like they were? I'm in Phoenix. I think it's the fifth largest city in the nation, and things have been changing. Over the last 60 to 75 days there's been a little change in weather, let's say, and why is that? Well, I'm going to tell you a couple of reasons.

I know people out there are saying, "Well, it's because interest rates have gone up." I'm going to give you some numbers on the interest rates. I'm also going to give you guys some more numbers on inventory, how inventory has gone up and why that is when people are still out there saying they can't find deals.

Why aren't homes flying off the shelves? That's the

number one complaint I'm getting right now from students all across the country from New York, Philadelphia, all the way to California. They're asking, "What am I doing wrong? Am I marketing this right? Is there the right terminology in the MLS listing? Is all the money gone? What's happening? I've had this home on the market for 42 days and only one offer, which wasn't even acceptable. I've had this on the market for 30 days already and haven't got an offer."

First of all, let's stop right there. I think over the last year or so experienced investors have gotten very comfortable with what has been happening in the market with our quick sales. There was a time up until about 60 days ago that if you got a deal and you put some decent money into it and put it back on the retail market, it was gone in a day. The same day you listed it, you'd have three, four, five offers minimum.

We've had 10 offers on certain homes, and we got very comfortable with that.

We have to be wary as real estate investors, because we all saw what happened back in the early and mid-2000s. We need to look at the comfort we have when little things change like interest rates. If you pay attention to politics—which, by the way, I don't pay a ton of attention to but I payenough to know a little bit about what's going on—there are people who get scared because of what possibly is going on with Syria.

Syria is the big news in politics right now. Some of those buyers, some of those sellers, some of those lenders, whoever they may be, are pulling back in the real estate market because they're a little scared about what's happening in Syria.

These are answers as to why the interest rates are going up.

Why are homes not flying off the shelves? We talked about the political reason in Syria, we talked about the interest rates going up; let's talk about the fact that the inventory has gone up. I ran numbers here in Phoenix; I didn't do it nationally. I know I have a lot of students who come from New York, Florida, all the way from California, but inventory has skyrocketed, just skyrocketed. Here in Phoenix we have seen the price point from $120,000 to $160,000 go up 20 percent. We've seen the price point of $160,000 to $200,000 go up 42 percent. We've seen $200,000 to $250,000 go up 39 percent and $250,000 to $300,000 go up a whopping 62 percent.

These numbers are real. The inventory is growing. Why is it growing and how does that affect us? It affects us when we're no longer the only deal on the market. Again, I just brought up the fact that we got very comfortable being able to get a deal, dump some good money into it, and sell it in a day because there's nothing else on the market for anyone to buy. Well, now inventory's gone up.

Now there are 19 percent, 42 percent, 62 percent increases in inventory. I will mention that a lot of that also correlates with closings. Closings have gone up, and rightly so. Homes are still affordable. People are still buying homes here in Phoenix, but whatever market you're in, because I have students from coast to coast, you need to know the inventory. How much has active inventory increased over the last 30 days? Look that up. Pay attention to that every 30 days. Know the numbers so you can make educated decisions.

What does that mean? Where did all of this inventory come from? Let's think about one thing: we've been going at a huge increase in value over the last year or year and a half all the way across the country. People are no longer underwater. They no longer have to short-sell their home. They may no longer be losing their home and they want to get out of it; they want it gone. That's one reason.

They may still not be employed, but the equity they've gained over the last year and half or so has gotten them out of being underwater and now there's actually equity. If they're able to sell at the price and the value the home has today, they might be able to pay off the bank in full with all interest due. That's one reason that there's more inventory: people want to get out from under their house. It's a burden. They still may be unemployed, but now they don't have to worry about it; they can sell it and make the bank whole and they don't have a short sale or a foreclosure on their credit score, and they're out from under the home.

What about the investors across the nation? A lot of investors are putting their homes up for market. There are a lot of investors who bought a home, didn't do anything to it, and put it to the market. Let's talk about the fact that over the last year and half, the values have been going up so much that people who simply own homes understand what happened in the early and mid-2000s.

They say, "This is the time to sell. Get me out now. I don't even need to sell but I want to because it's a good time to sell. People are dying for deals. People are dying to find homes. Inventory is low. Interest rates are low. Let me sell; good time to sell. Interest rates are going up; people are going to be a little bit scared. Let's not try to ride that; let's sell now while people are still pulling the trigger."

Let's bring up hedge funds for a second. Here in Phoenix we've been beaten to death by the hedge funds. It is an amazing feat that people like me and Eddie and several other very good investors here in Phoenix have been able to maintain and grow a business. We've grown year after year; every year in business we've grown, and over the last year and half or two years we've also seen hedge funds that have millions and billions of dollars to spend on inventory buying everything you can find.

I'll tell you a little story. We used to be at the auction very heavy back in 2011; probably 90 percent of our deals were bought at auction. Toward the end of 2011 and the beginning of 2012 we could not find a deal. We started freaking out, because all of a sudden our business model that had been so lucrative for us was going away because the hedge funds were here, killing us. They were overpaying by 110 percent, 120 percent of the value because the homes were great rental homes. They still worked for them. They were willing to overpay, especially for making a quick nickel on a fix-and-flip. They wanted to hold it so they could get 6 percent, 8 percent, 10 percent rate of return or a cap rate.

If you have hedge funds, you will realize they've pulled back. They are no longer buying as hot and heavy as they used to be. If they are still buying hot and heavy, if your market is a little bit behind Phoenix, which very well could be the case, be very wary. I don't work at these hedge funds myself, but I do have friends and colleagues who do, and they've told us that they're going to be pulling back.

Now things happen, and every day can change. I'm not predicting that by any means, but be very wary about the fact that hedge funds have pulled back, because when they pull back, inventory spikes again. They're not buying everything that's out there. In Phoenix they've pulled back over the last two months, and guess what, all of a sudden there's a lot more inventory. There's a lot more active inventory and there's a lot more inventory that's on the market for more than 30 days.

That's a very real situation. If you're in Atlanta, California, San Francisco, L.A., or Florida, and I think they're jumping into Ohio next, I'm telling you, you need to know about the hedge funds and you need to know when they're buying heavy and when they're going to pull back. That is a huge reason behind what's happening in the market.

Again, everyone keeps blaming the interest rates, but people don't think about these big hedge funds that have been buying millions if not billions of dollars' worth of real estate. Their pulling back now will increase the volume that is still in the market, which is a good thing.

When I'm teaching you marketing strategies, the economy is not quite as volatile as dropping or shooting straight up and gaining all this equity. You're going to have a little bit more of a normal 2 percent, 3 percent, 5 percent equity growth a year. People forget about those days. They forget about the history of our economy, which said the real estate market's going to gain 5 percent value every single year. They forget about the history of the real estate market and only remember the last 10 years or so that have been so brutal. Remember the hedge funds is a huge reason.

Let's talk about the interest rates and really get into it. We do a lot of deals on the fix-and-flip side. We are primarily looking for retail buyers. If you're wholesalers out there, I love wholesaling; I love being able to make the quick nickel over the slow dime. We absolutely wholesale; it's the smaller part of our business but we are wholesalers ourselves here in Phoenix. But 90 percent of our business is fix-and-flipping.

Let's talk about interest rates, because they affect our buyers. We are looking for the retail market; when interest rates jump, which everyone's been complaining about, it affects us. Let's use a big bank that a lot of individuals will get loans from, Wells Fargo. For a 30-year loan you can still get an interest rate in the mid 4s to low 5s. For a 15-year FHA loan you can still get an interest rate from the mid 3s, and for a 30-year jumbo loan, you can get it in the low to mid 4s. This is from Wells Fargo's website.

I'm not sure if you've ever personally purchased a home and gotten a home loan and I'm not sure how old you may be, but when I bought my first home in Northern California, I bought it at 6 percent interest. One loan, 100 percent financing from Wells Fargo, 6 percent interest for a $500,000 condo in Northern California. My payment every single month was $3,000. I was stoked. I loved it. I had to put nothing down and I got to pay $3,000 a month at 6 percent. Six percent was an awesome interest rate. I didn't even get close to 6 percent with the numbers I just presented.

Let me give you some more numbers. APR stands for annualized percentage rate. For a 30-year fixed loan, the interest rate is 4.375 percent. The APR is 4.96. APR includes the fees you would have to pay to get that interest rate. Your payment on a 4.96 APR is $1,026.97 on a $200,000 home. On a 30-year fixed FHA loan, your interest rate would be 4.125; your APR will be 5.598, so you're paying way more points on that loan and your payment would be $1,111.14.

That FHA loan is not even as good as just your 30-year fixed. Your 15-year fixed is the best one interestwise. You get a 3.375 interest rate; your APR or annualized percentage rate is 3.93, but your payments are $1,399.08. Why would your payments be more? That is the 15-year, not the 30-year.

Homes are still affordable; that's what I'm here to tell you. People are still buying. I don't want you out there saying, "My home's not selling because buyers are scared now and the interest rates are super high." I just read you Wells Fargo's interest rates. Not one of them was at 6 percent. The highest I read was 5.598 and that's because it's including the points you'd have to pay for the loan, but your mortgage would still be $1,111.14.

I don't want you all to sit there and blame the interest rates. It's just not true, and I had a meeting with a real estate agent who is very integrated with a couple of loan officers who say that 100 percent financing is coming back. I'm just the messenger, but I've heard that rumor. It may not be everywhere and it may not be for everybody, but I've heard it is absolutely coming back if it's not back already.

The interest rates are not the entire problem. I want you to take a step back and ask yourselves why there is high inventory. Why is inventory sitting on the market longer than one day? We got too used to that. We got too used to getting multiple offers within a day, two days, three days, four days, through a weekend. We started to sit back on our laurels and say, "There's no inventory." There was no inventory at all, so this is going to keep going until there is inventory, and then everyone wants to blame the interest rates for why buyers aren't buying. There is now more inventory. That is part of the reason you're not getting the buyers as quickly as you would like.

Interest rates do play a little bit of a game with people, because guess what: if you really can only afford $900 a month and your loan now is $1,026.97, you're not going to find the $126 every single month, right? You can't; you can really only afford $900. That's what your prequalification letter is for, to say what you can and can't afford. Of course the interest rates do play in, the economy does play in, unemployment does play in, and politics do play in, but let's not fool ourselves.

There are other variables out there as to why some of these homes aren't moving as fast as they used to move. We all know that short sales for the most part have gone away. People are gaining equity hand over fist over the last year. Short sales have gone away because you're no longer going to sell your home short of your loan. You're gaining equity, but as people gain equity, they realize they want to sell. They may not need to sell but they want out from under their home. Maybe they want some retirement money. Maybe they realize this is a good time to sell because of what we just went through with all the gaining of equity.

Realize that right now some of the bigger hedge funds are pulling back a little bit. They need to adjust; they need to account for their inventory and see what's out there, how much they have, what's rented, what type of returns they're getting. They're pulling back for a little while. I don't know when they're going to jump back in, I don't know how, and I don't know how heavy, but they'll jump back in somewhere. They won't spend those millions and billions of dollars just to disappear one day, and at the end of the day, people are getting equity. I go back to it: it's just a good time to get out from under a house.

What do we need to do as fix-and-flip investors? I know you're out there thinking, "Oh, okay, Justin. Thank you, I appreciate you at least explaining that it's not all the interest rates, but what do we need to do?" Well, we need to start adjusting the way we're buying deals. We need to look specifically at the numbers of days in market and at what price point.

How many of these properties are at $100,000 to $150,000? How many active over the last 30 days? How many closings? Do the same thing with the $150,000 to $200,000 and the $200,000 to $250,000. If you're in California, let's use $500,000: $500,000 to $550,000; $550,000 to $600,000; $600,000 to $650,000, and so on. Look at days on market, look at price points, and then look at closings, because if your days on market are high and your closings are low, that is not the price point you want to be flipping homes in.

If there aren't that many closings and your days on market are really high, that's just the price point. There's not a lot of buyers. I forgot the price point exactly, but I want to say it was $100,000 to $120,000 where there was an increase in inventory by, let's say, 20 percent but there was also an increase of closing by 40 percent. The increase doubled on closings from the increase on inventory. Twenty percent of inventory is a big number, but if you're going to add another 20 percent to that on the closings, that's a market I would strongly be looking at.

There are that many more buyers in that price point. Look at days on market. Look at the active inventory, meaning how many new active homes were listed on the MLS, and then how many closing happen in those 30 days? If you start doing that across certain price points, you may find a price point that will do exactly what I just explained. There may be 20 percent more inventory but there are 40 percent more closings, meaning the buyers are in that price point.

We need to go back to the drawing board. You need to act like you're a rookie investor—and if you are a rookie, this is exactly what you need to be doing—and look at the numbers. Where are the buyers who are still buying homes, who can still afford a 30-year fixed, a 15-year FHA, or whatever loan that they get?

Another thing that we have to do as fix-and-flippers is account for cost of money. Plenty of students are out there complaining, "Oh my god, this deal was so good but now I've held it for 60 days and the cost of money is so high and I'm spending 18 percent on my interest rate. It was a hard money loan and I'm already spending $2,500, $3,000 a month for this loan and it's just eating all my profit away. What happens if it's on the market for another four or five months? I'm going to end up losing money on this home."

I'm hearing that. Week after week I'm getting these emails and people are asking me these questions. You need to adjust how you account for your money. When you run your numbers, are you running them with holding cost for two months or are you running them with six months? Huge difference, right? If you're paying $3,000 for your money in holding cost and you have to hold that for six months, that's $18,000.

You need to account for your money, because if you're only holding that for two months, it's $6,000. Start adjusting how you run those numbers. You can't just assume that you're going to be able to sell a home in two months anymore. That used to be the case, but we know we should be looking at the numbers. We know it.

We should be accounting for a longer time of holding, but we get so excited and involved with the market and what it's doing and how many offers we get on the first day that we stop accounting for holding it for six months. Get back to that. Start accounting for holding for six months, cost of money, your taxes, commissions, whatever it may be. Those holding and closing costs need to be adjusted. That's what you can do as the fix-and-flip investor. That's what's going to help you.

I'll repeat those two major things. It all goes back to the

numbers. First, find the price point in which the closing percentage is higher than the increase in inventory, because that's where your buyers are. That's still a good market to play in. Go back to the numbers. Find where those closings are happening. What zip code? What price point?

Secondly, be a businessman. Go back to doing it the right way. Understand that it may take up to six months for you to close a flip.

If you can't hold that home for six months, do not buy it. Calculate your cost of money. Calculate your closing cost. Calculate all of your closing cost and holding cost, power, water, utilities, taxes, updating the yard every two or three weeks. Put that in there, spending $50 or $100 a month for someone to keep the yards and the pools clean, because it may sit on the market a little bit longer than we're used to.

Tomorrow this all could change. That's the great part about being a real estate investor. You've got to be flexible, you've got to ride the waves, and when you know the wave is going down or the wave is getting too big, get onto a different wave. Get creative. This is what I really excel at. I start getting creative in figuring out ways to find different deals that make us a profit. What areas, what zip codes, what price points, where the buyers are, how I get cheaper money—all of those things are what I focus on and what you guys should be focusing on as well.

What's Next?

Did You Enjoy The Book?

Let me know by leaving an honest review on Amazon.com. It helps to let other readers know that you got real value and helps communicate with me. I read every single review, sometimes multiple times.

For a special Thank You message and free bonus, visit

www.TheScienceOfFlipping.com

Justin Colby, Author

39363724R00080

Made in the USA
Lexington, KY
20 February 2015